KIDS ONLY!

QUIZZES

THE QUIZ BOOK COMPANY

First published in 2004 by
The Quiz Book Company Ltd
Bardfield Centre,
Great Bardfield, Essex, CM7 4SL

ISBN 1-84236-507-X

Printed in India

Some of the material in this book has been used previously
in Quiz Time. Other questions written by Chris Rigby.

QUIZ 1

· ·

1 The star sign of Gemini is represented by a pair
   of what?

2 What seven-letter H word is the name of a leather
   case for holding a pistol or revolver?

3 How many meanings does a double
   entendre have?

4 What do you call the tall, decorated wooden
   pillars carved by Native Americans?

5 Which alcoholic drink is also the name given to
   the left side of a ship?

6 What is the American equivalent of a Russian
   cosmonaut?

7 What instrument is named after the Greek
   god Pan?

8 Nag is a slang term for what animal?

9 What type of weapon is a cutlass?

10 What type of boat is steered by a gondolier?

ANSWERS

1. Twins 2. Holster 3. Two 4. Totem poles 5. Port 6. Astronaut 7. Pan pipes
8. Horse 9. A short curved sword 10. Gondola

QUIZ 2

. . . .

1 Which alcoholic drink is made from crushed grapes?

2 What is the name for the stick carried by a British policeman or woman?

3 Which transport machine has forks, gears and a chainwheel?

4 Which British palace is famous for its maze?

5 Who is the cartoon and comic strip sailor who loves spinach?

6 What is a male elephant called?

7 How many letters are there in the English (Roman) alphabet?

8 Is a great bustard an old-fashioned gun, a bird or a type of drink?

9 Sombrero and deerstalker are types of what?

10 In which city would you find the shop Harrods?

ANSWERS

1. Wine 2. Truncheon 3. Bicycle 4. Hampton Court 5. Popeye 6. Bull 7. 26
8. A bird 9. Hat 10. London

QUIZ 3

1 Who was the captain of the England rugby team in the 2003 World Cup?

2 An American quarter is worth how many cents?

3 What is the Japanese art of bonsai?

4 In which country was a wok first used for cooking?

5 Which chain store uses the brand name St Michael?

6 What sort of food is a courgette?

7 What colour are taxis in New York City?

8 Which part of a bishop's clothing is his mitre?

9 Are all metals magnetic?

10 When were the Olympics last held in Britain?

ANSWERS

1. Martin Johnson 2. 25 3. Growing miniature trees 4. China 5. Marks and Spencer 6. A vegetable 7. Yellow 8. His hat 9. No 10. 1948

QUIZ 4

1. An American dime is worth how many cents?

2. What type of fish is Bruce in the animated movie *Finding Nemo*?

3. Who was captain of the England cricket team before Nasser Hussein?

4. Ash Wednesday is the first day of which religious period?

5. Which is the most westerly country: Norway, Sweden or Finland?

6. Who wrote the play *Troilus and Cressida*?

7. What is the time that a baby spends inside its mother's womb called?

8. Who was selected as Labour Party candidate for Mayor of London in 2000?

9. If you were born on April 5th, which star sign would you be?

10. On which part of the body do cowboys wear chaps?

ANSWERS

1. Ten 2. Great White shark 3. Alec Stewart 4. Lent 5. Norway
6. Shakespeare 7. Gestation period or pregnancy 8. Frank Dobson
9. Aries 10. Legs

QUIZ 5

● ●

1　How many weeks are there in a year?

2　Red sky at night is whose delight?

3　From which country do lasagne and spaghetti come?

4　Where are bodies buried?

5　What relation is Prince Charles to Prince Philip?

6　How many tens are there in a thousand?

7　How many television channels for all viewers does the BBC fund?

8　Which part of the coffee plant is harvested to make the drink?

9　In Britain, which buildings have blue lamps outside them?

10　Which is longer: a foot or a yard?

ANSWERS

1. 52 2. Shepherds' 3. Italy 4. In a graveyard 5. Son 6. 100 7. Two 8. The beans 9. Police stations 10. A yard

QUIZ 6

. . . .

1 What was the first name of the composer Beethoven?

2 Which charity organises Red Nose Day?

3 With which sport is Nick Skelton associated?

4 What sort of creature is a tarantula?

5 Who played the title role in *The Vicar of Dibley*?

6 Which was the fastest airliner in the world?

7 Which car-maker's previous models include the *Capri* and the *Anglia*?

8 In which street is the prime minister's official London residence?

9 In which country is the world's longest wall?

10 How many English kings have been named Edward?

ANSWERS

1. Ludwig 2. Comic Relief 3. Horse jumping 4. A spider 5. Dawn French
6. Concorde 7. Ford 8. Downing Street 9. China 10. Eight

QUIZ 7

1 What is the name of the bank where Harry Potter keeps his wizard money?

2 Which band played a New Year's Eve night concert at Cardiff's Millennium Stadium?

3 Whose assembly line revolutionized car-making in the early 1900s?

4 What is the connection between *Wayne's World* and *Austin Powers: International Man of Mystery*?

5 How many make up a score?

6 Who was the most famous marshall of the wild west town of Tombstone?

7 What is the name for the regular rise and fall of the sea?

8 Which athletics commentator hosted *A Question of Sport* before Sue Barker?

9 In which year of the 1980s did a great storm cause much damage and destroy many trees in southern England?

10 How many birth signs are there in the zodiac?

ANSWERS

1. Gringott's 2. Manic Street Preachers 3. Henry Ford 4. Mike Myers wrote and starred in both 5. 20 6. Wyatt Earp 7. Tide 8. David Coleman 9. 1987 10. 12

QUIZ 8

1 How many lungs does the human body contain?

2 Which phone number is usually dialled for the emergency services in Britain?

3 What are the three emergency services?

4 In cockney rhyming slang, what does 'apples and pears' mean?

5 Where would you find woofers and tweeters?

6 If you were born on March 7th, what would your star sign be?

7 Can you give the first name of Victoria and David Beckham's first son?

8 What are Danish blue, Brie and Gouda examples of?

9 What colour was the Beatles' submarine?

10 Which soap has a pub called the Rovers Return?

ANSWERS

1. Two 2. 999 3. Police, Fire and Ambulance 4. Stairs 5. Loudspeakers
6. Pisces 7. Brooklyn 8. Cheeses 9. Yellow 10. *Coronation Street*

QUIZ 9

1 In which city would you find Madison Square Gardens?

2 Which airline sponsored the London Eye ride in London?

3 Was the Spanish Main in the Caribbean, Red or Mediterranean Sea?

4 How many make up a baker's dozen?

5 Which ancient people wore togas?

6 Which British city sits on the river Lagan?

7 How is $1^3/_5$ expressed as a decimal number?

8 Who did the knights of the Round Table serve?

9 Which tree gives its name to the syrup poured over pancakes?

10 In which TV soap did Dirty Den, Arthur Fowler and Laura Beala once appear?

ANSWERS

1. New York City 2. British Airways 3. Caribbean 4. 13 5. Romans 6. Belfast
7. 1.6 8. King Arthur 9. Maple 10. *EastEnders*

QUIZ 10

. . . .

1 What does a numismatist study?

2 Which player aimed a kung-fu kick at a Crystal Palace supporter and was then banned?

3 Who is the quiz master on *Countdown*?

4 What is the first letter of the Greek alphabet?

5 From which vegetable is sauerkraut made?

6 What does 'simultaneously' mean?

7 What is the square root of 121?

8 In which city were houses first given numbers?

9 Which language is described as Hispanic?

10 Which European city is famous for its Oktoberfest?

ANSWERS

1. Coins 2. Eric Cantona 3. Richard Whiteley 4. Alpha 5. Cabbage 6. At the same time 7. 11 8. Paris 9. Spanish 10. Munich

QUIZ 11

. . . .

1   Which precious stone is red?

2   Pikachu is a character in which cartoon series?

3   How many five pences in a pound?

4   What is a winklepicker: a bird, a tool for eating shellfish or a shoe?

5   If you were using split shot on a line tied with a size 16 hook, what would you be doing?

6   Is a minidisk: a way of storing computer information or music?

7   Name the board game that you would be playing if you landed on Mayfair?

8   What is the ninth letter of the alphabet?

9   How many sevens are there in 35?

10   How many sides does a dice have?

ANSWERS

1. A ruby 2. *Pokémon* 3. 20 4. A shoe 5. Fishing (angling) 6. Music
7. Monopoly 8. I 9. Five 10. Six

QUIZ 12

• •

1   In cockney rhyming slang, what is a 'trouble and strife'?

2   Of what are granny, reef and sheepshank examples?

3   In which boy band did Robbie Williams used to be?

4   Where would you be most likely to find an alternator?

5   What was the name of the sheep in *Wallace and Gromit*?

6   Lord Baden Powell founded which movement?

7   In the Bible, how many apostles did Jesus have?

8   An early version of what machine was called a 'boneshaker'?

9   Which substance makes bread rise?

10 With which sort of drink is the campaign group CAMRA associated?

ANSWERS

1. A wife 2. Knots 3. Take That 4. In a car engine 5. Shaun 6. Scouts
7. 12 8. Bicycle 9. Yeast 10. Real ale (beer)

QUIZ 13

· ·

1 According to the old phrase, what did curiosity do the cat?

2 In which daytime quiz show does Carol Vorderman star?

3 If you were born on December 27th, what would your star sign be?

4 If you were performing a cascade or shower, what pastime would you be taking part in?

5 What name did the ancient Greeks give to a supposed large island west of Gibraltar?

6 What number does the Roman numeral M equal?

7 What is the last letter of the Greek alphabet?

8 What is mulligatawny?

9 In which film did Tommy Lee Jones and Will Smith fight aliens?

10 Chelsea, Spode and Royal Doulton are types of what?

ANSWERS

1. Kill it 2. *Countdown* 3. Capricorn 4. Juggling 5. Atlantis 6. 1,000
7. Omega 8. A soup 9. *Men in Black* 10. Porcelain

QUIZ 14

• •

1　What is 1.25 expressed as a fraction?

2　What is the main ingredient of an omelette?

3　Which boy band's former lead singer was Ronan Keating?

4　What is the national airline of Canada?

5　Used in World War II, what sort of device were U-boats?

6　With which films do you associate Darth Maul and Darth Vader?

7　What does the French word 'bonjour' mean?

8　How many days are there in the month of April?

9　What would you do with a melon ball: eat it, kick it or fish with it?

10　How many 10-pence pieces are there in 20 pounds?

ANSWERS

1. 1¹/₄ 2. Eggs 3. Boyzone 4. Air Canada 5. Submarines 6. *Star Wars*
7. 'Hello' or 'good day' 8. 30 9. Eat it 10. 200

QUIZ 15

. . . .

1   Is oxtail soup made from an ox's tail?

2   What is the name of the actor who plays Pauline
    Fowler in *EastEnders*?

3   Which country was once ruled by tsars?

4   What does the French word 'oeuf' mean in
    English?

5   Which Michael Jackson video was the most
    expensive ever made?

6   In cockney rhyming slang, what is a 'frog and
    toad'?

7   Which was the first Boeing jet airliner?

8   How old is a centenarian?

9   What sport does Prince Charles play on horseback
    using a mallet?

10 If you were at a bureau de change what would
    you be doing?

ANSWERS

1. Yes 2. Wendy Richards 3. Russia 4. Egg 5. 'Thriller' 6. Road 7. Boeing 707
8. 100 9. Polo 10. Changing money into a different currency

QUIZ 16

. . . .

1   Who wrote tales about Flopsy, Mopsy and Cottontail?

2   What is a chow?

3   Which national radio station did Chris Evans once present on and have shares in?

4   What word means a type of pig meat and an amateur radio operator?

5   Which building traditionally has three balls displayed outside?

6   Who had a hit with 'No Scrubs' in 1999?

7   What is the national airline of Indonesia?

8   Was the Battle of Inkerman in the Crimean, Boer or Falklands War?

9   In which city did Anne Frank live when she wrote her famous diary?

10 In which month does the grouse-shooting season start in Britain?

ANSWERS

1. Beatrix Potter 2. A breed of dog 3. Virgin Radio 4. Ham
5. A pawnbrokers 6. TLC 7. Garuda 8. Crimean 9. Amsterdam 10. August

QUIZ 17

- -

1 What does the Roman numeral V equal?

2 Which is the higher belt in judo: black or yellow?

3 *Beetle*, *Golf* and *Polo* are types of car made by which motor manufacturer?

4 How many hours are in two days?

5 In what structure would Clark Kent change into Superman?

6 How many years of marriage are celebrated by a silver wedding?

7 What colour is the gemstone ruby?

8 Which popular author is the sister of actress Joan Collins?

9 Emulsion and enamel are types of what?

10 How many eighths are there in a half?

ANSWERS

1. Five 2. Black 3. Volkswagen (VW) 4. 48 5. A telephone box or booth
6. 25 7. Red 8. Jackie Collins 9. Paint 10. Four

QUIZ 18

• •

1 According to folklore, what does the sandman help children to do?

2 Who hosted the TV show *Blind Date*?

3 Which Greek philosopher was made to commit suicide by drinking hemlock?

4 What does the phrase 'Parlez-vous anglais?' mean in English?

5 In which European country is the port of Antwerp?

6 Which TV show has been hosted by Johnny Vaughn, Mark Little, Peter Kay and Chris Evans?

7 Which English king was killed at the Battle of Bosworth in 1485?

8 What can be divided into stanzas: time, food or poetry?

9 The moons Oberon and Miranda orbit which planet?

10 Which language was invented to be universal?

ANSWERS

1. Go to sleep 2. Cilla Black 3. Socrates 4. 'Do you speak English?'
5. Belgium 6. *The Big Breakfast* 7. Richard III 8. Poetry 9. Uranus
10. Esperanto

QUIZ 19

• •

1   What do the initials AWOL stand for in the military?

2   In which year of the 1900s was the bikini invented?

3   What unusual pet did the Roman emperor Julius Caesar have?

4   Nick Park is behind which popular animated characters made of modelling clay?

5   Is Ezra a book of the Old or New Testament?

6   The astrological sign Cancer is shown as what type of creature?

7   What day of the week does the German word 'Dienstag' refer to?

8   Who is the lead singer of the Manic Street Preachers?

9   In which country is Vesuvius found?

10   What word means both 'to invent' and 'cosmetics'?

ANSWERS

1. Absent With Out Leave 2. 1946 3. Giraffe 4. *Wallace and Gromit*
5. Old Testament 6. A crab 7. Tuesday 8. James Dean Bradfield 9. Italy
10. Make-up

QUIZ 20

1 Which K word is another term for tomato sauce?

2 Which device, currently orbiting Earth, was named after the astronomer Edwin Hubble?

3 Are Airbus aircraft made by a group of American, European or Asian companies?

4 Did Alex Ferguson become manager of Manchester United in 1986, 1993 or 1996?

5 St Clare is the patron saint of television. True or false?

6 What is 0.75 expressed as a fraction?

7 Of what are bourbon, digestive and malted milk examples?

8 Which colour has shades known as scarlet and vermilion?

9 How many threes are there in 63?

10 In paints, which two colours are mixed to make green?

ANSWERS

1. Ketchup 2. The Hubble Space Telescope 3. European 4. 1986 5. True
6. $^3/_4$ 7. Biscuits 8. Red 9. 21 10. Blue and yellow

QUIZ 21

1 Is a sole a freshwater or saltwater fish?

2 How many years of marriage does a golden wedding celebrate?

3 Which former Spice Girl sang on a hit single with Bryan Adams?

4 In the nursery rhyme, which town was Dr Foster heading to: Towcester, Gloucester or Worcester?

5 Which trade did Jesus learn?

6 If you were born in February, which gem would be your birthstone?

7 What item of clothing is a homburg?

8 Which cartoon pirate has an enemy called Black Jake?

9 In French it is 'jeudi', in German it is 'Donnerstag'. What day of the week is it in English?

10 In imperial measurements, how many pints equal a UK gallon?

ANSWERS

1. Saltwater 2. 50 3. Mel C 4. Gloucester 5. Carpentry 6. Amethyst 7. A hat
8. Captain Pugwash 9. Thursday 10. Eight

QUIZ 22

· ·

1 What does a male cygnet grow up to be?

2 What number do people dial in the United States for emergency services?

3 In Roman numerals, what number is represented by CXXXVII?

4 Which TV show launched the career of actor/singer Will Smith?

5 Which British building traditionally has a red-and-white striped pole displayed outside?

6 Who is the quiz master on *University Challenge*?

7 Where is the Prime Meridian situated?

8 The *Niña*, the *Pinta* and the *Santa Maria* were the three ships in the voyage commanded by which famous explorer?

9 What is the main vegetable ingredient of the Russian soup, borscht?

10 Where would you find derailleur gears?

ANSWERS

1. Cob or male swan 2. 911 3. 137 4. *The Fresh Prince of Bel Air* 5. A barber shop 6. Jeremy Paxman 7. Greenwich 8. Christopher Columbus 9. Beetroot 10. On a bicycle

QUIZ 23

1 What sort of animal was often killed with a harpoon?

2 What do the initials NHS stand for?

3 Is A6 paper bigger than A5?

4 Which science-fiction film starred Ewan McGregor as a Jedi Knight?

5 What is a museum of the stars called?

6 What sort of animal is a pug?

7 In a pack of cards, does the queen of clubs look to her left or right?

8 How can you tell that a car is driven by a learner?

9 What colour is a canary?

10 If you walk up something do you ascend or descend?

ANSWERS

1. A whale 2. National Health Service 3. No, it is half the size of A5
4. *Star Wars Episode 1: The Phantom Menace* 5. Planetarium 6. A dog 7. Left
8. By the L-plate signs displayed on the car 9. Yellow 10. Ascend

QUIZ 24

1 How many years have a couple been married if they are celebrating their diamond wedding?

2 Which female singer was with the Fugees before having solo success?

3 In Roman numerals, what number is represented by CXIII?

4 What are the first names of the two Geordie lads who hosted *I'm a Celebrity, Get Me Outta Here* on Saturday mornings?

5 What was the stage name of the pair when they were a singing duo?

6 If you were born in January, what gem would be your birthstone?

7 Is the currency of China: the Yuan, the Yen or the Yinni?

8 How many people usually make up a jury in England and Wales?

9 What kind of food comes from Bakewell?

10 What word is both a harbour and a socket on the back of a personal computer?

ANSWERS

1. 60 2. Lauryn Hill 3. 113 4. Ant and Dec 5. PJ and Duncan 6. Garnet
7. Yuan 8. 12 9. A tart 10. Port

QUIZ 25

. . . .

1 According to Chinese tradition, was the year 2000 the year of the cat, the monkey or the dragon?

2 If you were born on the October 1, which star sign would you be?

3 In Roman numerals, what number is represented by XIX?

4 Which TV soap does singer Adam Rickett star in?

5 In which English county would you find Matlock?

6 What date is St Stephen's feast day?

7 In computing, what does USB stand for?

8 What is the currency of Pakistan?

9 In which Dutch city does the International Court of Justice sit?

10 The Asian country of Cambodia was formerly known as what?

ANSWERS

1. Year of the dragon 2. Libra 3. 19 4. *Coronation Street* 5. Derbyshire
6. December 26th 7. Universal Serial Bus 8. Rupee 9. The Hague
10. Kampuchea

QUIZ 26

. . . .

1   Which year was the last ever Five Nations rugby union tournament played?

2   What are the two red suits in a pack of cards?

3   Which fruit, beginning with A, is similar in shape to a small peach?

4   Which tennis tournament is famous for strawberries and cream and its Centre Court?

5   Does the word 'amplify' mean to make sound louder or quieter?

6   Which British mammal lives in a sett and has a distinctive black-and-white striped head?

7   If you 'bottle up' your feelings, what do you do with them?

8   Is the first book of the Bible, Exodus, Genesis or Psalms?

9   How many sides does a 50-pence piece have?

10 What is the past tense of the word 'drink'?

ANSWERS

1. 1999 2. Hearts and diamonds 3. Apricot 4. Wimbledon 5. Louder
6. Badger 7. Keep them to yourself 8. Genesis 9. Seven 10. Drank

QUIZ 27

. . . .

1 What does 'in the buff' mean?

2 Which animal represents the star sign Taurus?

3 Which ex-American president was nicknamed Tricky Dicky?

4 In the nursery rhyme, what could Jack Sprat's wife not eat?

5 Who wrote and directed the *Star Wars* films?

6 What sort of aircraft were the Lancaster and the Stirling?

7 Which type of instrument are Gibson, Les Paul and Fender famous for making?

8 What flavour is the drink crème de menthe?

9 Chiropody is the treatment of which part of your body?

10 What is the square root of 64?

ANSWERS

1. Naked 2. A bull 3. Richard Nixon 4. Fat 5. George Lucas 6. Bombers (from World War II) 7. Electric guitars 8. Mint 9. Your feet 10. Eight

QUIZ 28

1 If you had MP3 files running through a player, what would you be doing?

2 What is the more commonly used name for the musical instrument known as timpani?

3 What is the chemical symbol for chlorine?

4 Which H word means 'New Year's Eve' in Scotland?

5 What is the highest female voice called?

6 How many revolutions per minute does an LP record turn at?

7 St Bona is the patron saint of air hostesses. True or false?

8 What name is given to a creature that lives on another animal and gets its food from it?

9 The World War II Battle of the Leyte Gulf was between Japan and which other country?

10 Slick Willie is the nickname of which United States president?

ANSWERS

1. Listening to music downloaded form the Internet 2. Kettle drum 3. Cl
4. Hogmanay 5. Soprano 6. 33 and $1/3$ 7. True 8. Parasite 9. The United
States 10. Bill Clinton

QUIZ 29

1 Which person sells houses and other properties?

2 Around which part of your body might you wear a dicky bow?

3 What is the opposite of temporary: infinite, enormous or permanent?

4 Were tea bags invented in the 1420s, the 1620s or the 1920s?

5 From which country does Liebfraumilch wine come?

6 Are the Prodigy a dance music act, a comedy sketch team or an American basketball team?

7 What relation is the brother of your father to you?

8 For which national side has Colin Hendry played football?

9 Which are the largest of all plants: seaweeds, trees or cacti?

10 Where would you find a meteorite: underwater, in a desert or in space?

ANSWERS

1. An estate agent 2. Your neck 3. Permanent 4. 1920s 5. Germany
6. A dance music act 7. Your uncle 8. Scotland 9. Trees 10. In space

QUIZ 30

1 Is a *cor anglais* a woodwind, stringed or percussion instrument?

2 What name is given to a small, round beetle with black spots on its red wings?

3 What are you, if you are laid back?

4 What sort of drink is Adam's Ale?

5 Which is the largest stringed instrument?

6 About what subject is the quiz show *They Think It's All Over*?

7 Is the tale of Daniel and the lions in the Old or New Testament of the Bible?

8 Which animal represents the star sign Capricorn?

9 How old do you have to be to hold a full driving licence in Britain?

10 Where is the sting of a scorpion situated?

ANSWERS

1. Woodwind 2. Ladybird 3. Relaxed 4. Water 5. Harp 6. Sport 7. Old Testament 8. A goat 9. 17 10. In its tail

QUIZ 31

1 In Greek mythology, who was set 12 labours?

2 In Roman numerals, what number is represented by XXXIX?

3 Which F word means accidental success?

4 Of which country did Albert Einstein become a citizen in 1901?

5 Is a leveret a young rabbit, hare or ferret?

6 What is the largest brass instrument?

7 Juno and Gold beaches were landing points for which World War II invasion?

8 How many American senators are elected from each US state?

9 Name the first of the *Wallace and Gromit* films?

10 Is the Sun a thousand, a million or 100 million times bigger than Earth?

ANSWERS

1. Hercules 2. 39 3. Fluke 4. Switzerland 5. A young hare 6. The tuba
7. D-Day (Normandy landings) 8. Two 9. *A Grand Day Out* 10. A million

QUIZ 32

• •

1 How many sides has a 20-pence piece?

2 If you fixed water pipes in a house, what would your job title be?

3 Poodles were once used as hunting dogs. True or false?

4 Who were the first people to live in New Zealand: Maoris, Aboriginals or the Spanish?

5 What is the American spelling of 'grey'?

6 How many strings does a violin have?

7 Which two paint colours would you mix to make purple?

8 If you serve a double fault, which sport are you playing?

9 Which word means a small downpour of rain and also a bathroom spray device?

10 In which continent is the country Togo situated?

ANSWERS

1. Seven 2. A plumber 3. True 4. Maoris 5. Gray 6. Four 7. Red and blue
8. Tennis 9. Shower 10. Africa

QUIZ 33

. . . .

1 Who, in the Bible, was swallowed alive by a whale?

2 Does the musical term *adagio* mean fast, bass or very slow?

3 If you were born in April, what gem would be your birthstone?

4 What is the name of a building used to store aircraft?

5 What do the initials VAT stand for?

6 What creature would you be eating if you were served calimari?

7 What food, made from a stuffed sheep's stomach, is often eaten on Burn's Night?

8 What does the word 'utterly' mean?

9 Which day of the week is called 'Mittwoch' in German?

10 If you are wily, are you tall and thin, rude or cunning?

ANSWERS

1. Jonah 2. Very slow 3. Diamond 4. Hangar 5. Value Added Tax 6. Squid
7. Haggis 8. Completely 9. Wednesday 10. Cunning

QUIZ 34

1 Is contralto the highest or lowest female voice?

2 Which Moroccan port gives its name to the fruit, the tangerine?

3 About which subject is the quiz show *Never Mind The Buzzcocks*?

4 Riga is the capital of Latvia, Lithuania or Estonia?

5 The TV show *Stars in Their Eyes* is hosted by which Kelly: Lorraine, Gene or Matthew?

6 If you were born in May, what gem would be your birthstone?

7 Sir Alf Ramsey managed which English sports team in the 1960s?

8 Nassau is the capital of Bermuda, the Bahamas or Trinidad and Tobago?

9 If you were born on June 18th, what would be your star sign?

10 If you cook something in a pastry case, would your dish be en croute, al fresco or pot au feu?

ANSWERS

1. The lowest 2. Tangiers 3. Pop music 4. Latvia 5. Matthew 6. Emerald
7. Football team 8. The Bahamas 9. Gemini 10. En croute

QUIZ 35

• •

1   Does the rice dish risotto come from India, Wales or Italy?

2   Which Sheriff was an enemy of Robin Hood?

3   With what type of appliance is the name Dyson associated?

4   Who was born Elizabeth Alexandra Mary of Windsor?

5   Were the Velvet Underground a pop music band, a terrorist group or a group of modern artists?

6   What type of body part are biceps and triceps?

7   What is 0.5 of 11?

8   What is someone who sells fruit and vegetables called?

9   Which foodstuff could be UHT, condensed or semi-skimmed?

10 What is 20 percent of 200?

ANSWERS

1. Italy 2. Sheriff of Nottingham 3. Vacuum cleaner 4. Queen Elizabeth II
5. A pop music band 6. Muscles 7. 5.5 8. A greengrocer 9. Milk 10. 40

QUIZ 36

• •

1 According to the grammatical rule, which letter always comes before 'e', except after 'c'?

2 If you cook food slowly in a covered pan are you braising it, flash-frying it or blanching it?

3 In the Vietnam War, did the United States join the side of the South or North Vietnamese forces?

4 David Trimble is a politician in which part of the United Kingdom?

5 What nationality was the composer Richard Wagner?

6 Was Caligula a Viking warlord, a Saxon king or a Roman emperor?

7 Is hypothermia when your body gets very hot, very cold or lacking water?

8 Which melon has pink flesh and lots of large black seeds?

9 Which is the world's most popular sport?

10 What name is given to a fertile place in a desert?

ANSWERS

1. 'i' 2. Braising 3. South Vietnam 4. Ulster (Northern Ireland) 5. German
6. Roman emperor 7. Very cold 8. Watermelon 9. Football 10. Oasis

QUIZ 37

1 Anne of Burgundy was the first woman to receive which sign of an impending marriage?

2 How old was Sir Stanley Matthews when he stopped playing professional football?

3 How old was he when he died in February 2000?

4 What was the last album the Beatles made: 'Sgt Pepper's Lonely Hearts Club Band', 'Abbey Road' or 'Let It Be'?

5 What name is given to a law judge's small wooden hammer?

6 Which London Underground line is coloured brown on a map?

7 In which year did Margaret Thatcher become British prime minister?

8 Was she the first ever female prime minister of Great Britain?

9 What are progeny: fragments of Moon rock, a class of virus or children?

10 What is the official language of Haiti?

ANSWERS

1. A diamond engagement ring 2. 50 3. 85 4. 'Let It Be' 5. A gavel
6. Bakerloo 7. 1979 8. Yes 9. Children 10. French

QUIZ 38

• •

1. In which James Bond film did the character Oddjob appear?

2. What is the name of the headquarters of the Metropolitan Police Force?

3. Which fish makes spectacular leaps upstream to return to its birthplace?

4. Who was the first Frenchman to manage Arsenal football club?

5. What are the horns of a stag called?

6. If someone is Oxbridge-educated, which university other than Oxford may they have attended?

7. What are *Pravda*, *The Washington Post* and *The Miami Herald*?

8. In which athletics event did Steve Backley once hold the world record?

9. Which European country has the continent's only active volcanoes?

10. Which garden creature starts life as a tadpole?

ANSWERS

1. *Goldfinger* 2. New Scotland Yard 3. The salmon 4. Arsene Wenger
5. Antlers 6. Cambridge 7. Newspapers 8. The javelin 9. Italy 10. Frog

QUIZ 39

. . . .

1 Which word means a type of fish and the bottom of a shoe?

2 What was the name of the house where Toad lived?

3 Who wrote *Macbeth* and *Twelfth Night*?

4 What kind of animal was Barbar?

5 What do sentences always start with?

6 Who was Romeo in love with?

7 What do the initials RIP stand for?

8 What sort of words are run, jump, talk and fall?

9 What is the name of the punctuation symbol used to provide a pause in a sentence?

10 What is the word 'fridge' short for?

ANSWERS

1. Sole 2. Toad Hall 3. William Shakespeare 4. An elephant 5. A capital letter 6. Juliet 7. Rest In Peace 8. Verbs 9. A comma 10. Refrigerator

QUIZ 40

．．．．．．．．．．．．．．．．．．．．．．．．．．．．．．

1. How many thieves were with Ali Baba?

2. What word is a flat-bottomed boat and a long kick of a football or rugby ball?

3. What is the meaning of the phrase 'to keep your nose clean'?

4. In the nursery rhyme, what did the cow jump over?

5. How are Porthos, Aramis and Athos collectively known?

6. Who marched his men up to the top of the hill?

7. Which letter can you add to 'ham' to make a word meaning false, fake or fictitious?

8. Who wrote the James Bond books?

9. What sort of animal was Tarka?

10. What is the plural of the word goose?

ANSWERS

1. 40 2. Punt 3. To stay out of trouble 4. The Moon 5. The Three Musketeers
6. The Grand Old Duke of York 7. S (sham) 8. Ian Fleming 9. An otter
10. Geese

QUIZ 41

1 Which famous poet recently re-wrote the ancient tale of Beowulf?

2 What word can mean 'to knock' and 'a sort of container'?

3 Who or what is shanks' pony?

4 Which brothers were famous for writing fairytales?

5 What is a cat o' nine tails?

6 Which word is a part of an elephant and the body of a tree?

7 Who wrote *A Brief History of Time*?

8 What special feature do words or phrases that are palindromes have?

9 What title did Sir John Betjeman hold for many years?

10 What does YMCA stand for?

ANSWERS

1. Seamus Heaney 2. Jar 3. To walk on foot 4. The Brothers Grimm
5. A form of whip 6. Trunk 7. Stephen Hawking 8. They read the same
forwards as they do backwards 9. Poet Laureate 10. Young Men's Christian
Association

QUIZ 42

1 What type of building holds books for public use?

2 Which doctor is famous for *Green Eggs and Ham* and other silly stories?

3 If schoolchildren play truant, what do they do?

4 Which bird is often given the nickname Polly?

5 What is the name of the dog in the *Peanuts* cartoon stories?

6 What type of animal is featured in *Watership Down*?

7 What word do Americans use to describe the boot of a car?

8 What job does Pat do in the books written by John Cunliffe?

9 What does the phrase 'to lose your marbles' mean?

10 What sort of book contains the spellings of words?

ANSWERS

1. A library 2. Dr Seuss 3. Stay away from school 4. A parrot 5. Snoopy
6. Rabbits 7. Trunk 8. He is a postman 9. To go mad 10. A dictionary

QUIZ 43

. . . .

1   Who wrote the book *Animal Farm*?

2   What word is an sherry-like alcoholic drink and a sort of harbour?

3   What do the initials NUS stand for?

4   Which nursery rhyme character ate curds and whey?

5   What is the past tense of steal?

6   What is the plural of wolf?

7   Is the phrase 'a Santa at Nasa' a palindrome?

8   Who was in wonderland and went through the looking-glass?

9   What do the initials NFA stand for?

10 Which book featured a man-child called Mowgli?

ANSWERS

1. George Orwell 2. Port 3. National Union of Students 4. Miss Muffet
5. Stole 6. Wolves 7. Yes 8. Alice 9. No Fixed Abode 10. *The Jungle Book*

QUIZ 44

• •

1. What word means a book written by a person about their life?

2. What does the Latin phrase *bona fide* mean?

3. Who is the child star of the books written by JK Rowling?

4. What grammatical term is 'Super Sam smashes Sampras' an example of?

5. What do the initials ESP stand for?

6. In *Tom's Midnight Garden*, who was Tom's friend from another age?

7. What word means a group of seals or whales?

8. How many *Hitch-Hiker's Guide to the Galaxy* books are there?

9. Which comedian co-wrote the *Blackadder* scripts with Richard Curtis?

10. Which word can be added to 'pet' to mean a floor covering?

ANSWERS

1. Autobiography 2. In good faith 3. Harry Potter 4. Alliteration
5. Extra-Sensory Perception 6. Hattie 7. A pod 8. Four 9. Ben Elton 10. Car

QUIZ 45

• •

1   What group of animals is called a pride?

2   Which children's book asked the reader to search for a character with a shortened version of the name Walter?

3   Who had a teddy bear nicknamed Winnie the Pooh?

4   What sort of stories are associated with the writer Hans Christian Andersen?

5   What do you do if you 'chance your arm'?

6   In the nursery rhyme, what were Jack and Jill going up the hill to get?

7   What does the abbreviation HMS stand for?

8   Which town is closely associated with William Shakespeare?

9   What type of creatures were Tomsk, Orinocho and Bungo?

10 What do the initials WWF stand for?

ANSWERS

1. Lions   2. *Where's Wally?*   3. Christopher Robin   4. Fairytales   5. Take a risk
6. A pail of water   7. His (or Her) Majesty's Ship   8. Stratford-upon-Avon
9. Wombles   10. World Wrestling Federation

QUIZ 46

• •

1 Who is the world's most successful horror writer, with books including *Misery*, *Rose Madder* and *The Shining*?

2 What was the name of Winnie the Pooh's small, pink friend?

3 What word can mean 'to hobble' and is used to describe something that is floppy?

4 In the Alice stories, what creature could be found asleep in a teapot?

5 Is a coracle a prophet, a council meeting place or a boat?

6 What word is a boy's name, a duck's beak and a note of the cost of something?

7 In the nursery rhyme, what was the king doing in his counting house?

8 Which early-reading series of books featured Pat the dog?

9 Who wrote *Sons and Lovers*?

10 In *Treasure Island*, who was Captain Flint?

ANSWERS

1. Stephen King 2. Piglet 3. Limp 4. A dormouse 5. A boat 6. Bill
7. Counting out his money 8. Peter and Jane 9. DH Lawrence 10. A parrot

QUIZ 47

· ·

1 Which poet wrote *The Waste Land*?

2 Which short word can you place after feather, flower and sick?

3 What word is used to describe a group of crows?

4 What does the abbreviation NSPCC stand for?

5 Who wrote the long-running play *The Mousetrap*?

6 Who wrote *The Silmarillion* and *The Hobbit*?

7 Which trilogy of books is the above author most renowned for?

8 What is the name of the dog in *Peter Pan*?

9 Who wrote the *Little House on the Prairie* stories?

10 In which classic book series would you find George and Timmy?

ANSWERS

1. TS Elliot 2. Bed 3. A murder 4. National Society for the Prevention of Cruelty to Children 5. Agatha Christie 6. JRR Tolkein 7. *The Lord of the Rings* 8. Nana 9. Laura Ingalls Wilder 10. *The Famous Five*

QUIZ 48

• •

1 Who did Fagin and the Artful Dodger take under their wing?

2 What do the initials UN stand for?

3 About what subject has Delia Smith written many successful books?

4 RL Stein writes what sort of book?

5 What does the phrase 'last gasp' mean?

6 What do the initials RSPB stand for?

7 What do the letters 'o.g.' stand for in football?

8 What would you call a group of birds?

9 In the nursery rhyme, how many birds were baked in a pie?

10 Which famous book character was described as 'a bear of very little brain'?

ANSWERS

1. Oliver Twist 2. United Nations 3. Cookery 4. Horror books for children and teenagers 5. Right at the end, or the last moment 6. Royal Society for the Protection of Birds 7. Own goal 8. A flock 9. 24 10. Winnie the Pooh

QUIZ 49

. . . .

1 What sorts of words are adjectives?

2 What do the initials TUC stand for?

3 Which famous author wrote *Bleak House*?

4 In which city was Shakespeare's Globe Theatre?

5 What book gives lists of words with similar meanings?

6 What name is found on the most common version of the above?

7 What does the abbreviation WWW stand for?

8 Which Brontë wrote *Wuthering Heights*?

9 Which letter can be added to the word 'loop' to make the name of a type of ship?

10 Which pop star's frank autobiography was called *Is That It*?

ANSWERS

1. Words that describe something 2. Trades Union Congress 3. Charles Dickens 4. London 5. A thesaurus 6. Roget's 7. World Wide Web 8. Emily 9. S (sloop) 10. Bob Geldof

QUIZ 50

• •

1. Which word means to have loaned someone something and is also a religious date on the calendar?

2. Which early-reading books featured a boy and girl with names that start with the letter J?

3. Is a braggart a boastful person, a part of a horse or a petty criminal such as a thief?

4. What is an antonym?

5. Can you give an antonym of miserly?

6. What is an antonym of risky?

7. Which author of over 500 romantic stories claimed to write each book in just seven days?

8. Which female author wrote the book on which the film *The Color Purple* was based?

9. With what sort of books was Wainwright associated?

10. Who wrote *The Canterbury Tales*?

ANSWERS

1. Lent 2. Janet and John 3. A boastful person 4. A word that means the opposite of another word 5. Generous 6. Safe 7. Barbara Cartland 8. Alice Walker 9. Walking guides 10. Chaucer

QUIZ 51

. . . .

1 Which children's book character has a friend called Big Ears?

2 Where did Little Jack Horner sit?

3 What letter can be added to the word hop to mean 'a store'?

4 Which letter is always followed by 'u' in English words?

5 Which creature finally eats Captain Hook?

6 Which letter can be added to hat to mean talk?

7 About what animal is the book *Black Beauty*?

8 Which boy wizard has stormed to fame in a series of books?

9 What are the five vowels?

10 Who wrote the *Famous Five* books?

ANSWERS

1. Noddy 2. In the corner 3. S (shop) 4. Q 5. A crocodile 6. C (chat)
7. A horse 8. Harry Potter 9. A E I O U 10. Enid Blyton

QUIZ 52

• •

1 What kind of creature was Bilbo Baggins?

2 Which fictional detective had an enemy called Moriarty?

3 Which famous detective's first appearance was in the book *The Mysterious Affair at Styles*?

4 What do the initials QC mean in law?

5 Who wrote tales about *Brer Rabbit*?

6 What two words, which sound the same but are spelt differently, mean certain and a beach?

7 Who is the boy who never grew up?

8 Which child's World War II diaries portrayed the horrors of racial persecution?

9 Who wrote the book *The Iron Man*?

10 In which horror story does Jonathan Harker hunt down a vampire?

ANSWERS

1. A hobbit 2. Sherlock Holmes 3. Hercule Poirot 4. Queen's Counsel
5. Uncle Remus 6. Sure and shore 7. Peter Pan 8. Anne Frank 9. Ted
Hughes 10. *Dracula*

QUIZ 53

. . . .

1 Who wrote the horror story *The Pit and the Pendulum*?

2 In which series of books would you find Ford Prefect and Arthur Dent?

3 Who wrote nonsense verse including the poem *The Owl and the Pussycat*?

4 What is a synonym?

5 Can you give a synonym of the word cheerful?

6 What is a synonym of the word gigantic?

7 Which English romantic poet wrote 'To Autumn', 'Ode to a Nightingale' and 'To Hope'?

8 Which famous sleuth played the violin and wore a deerstalker hat?

9 What would you be if you were accused of having 'short arms and deep pockets'?

10 Which famous writer has published books such as *The Running Man* under the pseudonym Richard Bachman?

ANSWERS

1. Edgar Allen Poe 2. *The Hitch-Hiker's Guide to the Galaxy* 3. Edward Lear
4. A word which means the same as another word 5. Happy 6. Huge
7. John Keats 8. Sherlock Holmes 9. Mean or miserly
10. Stephen King

QUIZ 54

1 Which Norse god gave his name to Thursday?

2 What do the initials PTO stand for?

3 What is the name of the first *Harry Potter* book?

4 What is the name of Harry's unusual school?

5 Who visits a chocolate factory in the Roald Dahl story?

6 Which fantasy author has written *Mort*, *Truckers* and *Dangerous Creatures*?

7 How many people speak in a monologue?

8 How do you feel if you are 'tickled pink'?

9 Which Charles wrote *Great Expectations*?

10 What type of animal is Spot?

ANSWERS

1. Thor 2. Please turn over 3. *Harry Potter and the Philosopher's Stone*
4. Hogwarts 5. Charlie 6. Terry Pratchett 7. One 8. Happy, delighted
9. Charles Dickens 10. A dog

QUIZ 55

• •

1 Who wrote *Oliver Twist*?

2 What word is given to the letters of the alphabet that are not vowels?

3 Did George Orwell or George Elliot write *The Road to Wigan Pier*?

4 Which satirical magazine was started by Peter Cook and others, and is edited by Ian Hislop?

5 Which famous lady detective was the star of a number of books written by Agatha Christie?

6 Who wrote the adventure story *Kidnapped*?

7 What term is used to describe a number of kangaroos?

8 What is the name of the system of organizing books found in most libraries?

9 What newspaper was nicknamed *The Thunderer*?

10 Which comedian wrote *Stark* and *Popcorn*?

ANSWERS

1. Charles Dickens 2. Consonants 3. George Orwell 4. *Private Eye* 5. Miss Marple 6. Robert Louis Stevenson 7. A troop 8. The Dewey Decimal System 9. *The Times* 10. Ben Elton

QUIZ 56

- -

1 What is the removable paper cover on many hardback books called?

2 Which comedian wrote *The Liar* and *Hippopotamus*?

3 Which word means 'to illustrate' and 'a tie in a contest'?

4 Past, future and present are examples of what part of grammar?

5 What is a pseudonym?

6 Which ex-Goon has written comic versions of *Black Beauty* and *Dracula*?

7 What was the title of Sir Alex Ferguson's best-selling autobiography?

8 How many does the prefix deci- signify?

9 Which mystery writer's books include *Death in the Air*, *The ABC Murders* and *Evil Under the Sun*?

10 Which annual prize for adult novels was won in 1999/2000 by an adaptation of *Beowulf*?

ANSWERS

1. Dust jacket 2. Stephen Fry 3. Draw 4. Tenses 5. A false name used by a writer 6. Spike Milligan 7. *Managing My Life* 8. Ten 9. Agatha Christie 10. The Whitbread Prize

QUIZ 57

1 What is the plural of the word sheep?

2 In the nursery rhyme, did Jack or Jill fall down the hill last?

3 Which bear came from Peru and was incredibly fond of marmalade?

4 Which word, meaning halt, rhymes with hop?

5 Which vegetable was turned into a carriage for Cinderella?

6 At what time did the carriage turn back into the vegetable?

7 Is a minuet a gun, a dance or a type of castle tower?

8 On which London common do the Wombles live?

9 Of which country is Robert Burns the national poet?

10 In the nursery rhyme, which old woman went to fetch her dog a bone?

ANSWERS

1. Sheep 2. Jill 3. Paddington 4. Stop 5. A pumpkin 6. Midnight 7. A dance
8. Wimbledon 9. Scotland 10. Old Mother Hubbard

QUIZ 58

• •

1 Which word is used to describe a group of hens?

2 Which book about four sisters was written by Louisa May Alcott?

3 What word describes a person turning pink with embarrassment?

4 Who wrote the book *Frankenstein*?

5 To which famous poet was the author of *Frankenstein* married?

6 Which fictional detective's last case was described in the book *Curtains*?

7 Which famous writer had her book *Pride and Prejudice* rejected by a number of publishers?

8 What word is used to describe a group of dancers?

9 What book about a young lord was written by Frances Hodgson Burnett?

10 Which female author wrote *Malory Towers*, *The Secret Island* and the *St Clare's Naughtiest Girl* series?

ANSWERS

1. A brood 2. *Little Women* 3. Blush 4. Mary Shelley 5. Percy Shelley
6. Hercule Poirot 7. Jane Austen 8. A troupe 9. *Little Lord Fauntleroy*
10. Enid Blyton

QUIZ 59

• •

1   What is the surname of Harry Potter's horrid Aunt and Uncle?

2   Which prolific author is in *The Guinness Book of Records* for writing 26 books in one year, 1983?

3   Which David wrote the award-winning *Skellig* and *Kit's Wilderness* novels for children?

4   What is a curmudgeon?

5   Which detective had a close friend called Captain Hastings?

6   Which writer and wit said 'I have nothing to declare but my genius'?

7   Which female writer, who died in 1817, wrote *Northanger Abbey* and *Mansfield Park*?

8   Where did the Pied Piper come from?

9   Which fairytale character had long golden hair?

10 According to the old saying, what does 'absence make'?

ANSWERS

1. Dursley 2. Barbara Cartland 3. David Almond 4. A bad-tempered person
5. Hercule Poirot 6. Oscar Wilde 7. Jane Austen 8. Hamelin 9. Rapunzel
10. 'The heart grow fonder'

QUIZ 60

1 What was the title of the second *Harry Potter* book?

2 Which ex-Goon wrote *Adolf Hitler: My Part in his Downfall* and *Milliganimals*?

3 What would you be if you were described as 'long in the tooth'?

4 For what sort of books is Mrs Beeton best known?

5 What word can mean 'a schoolchild' and part of the eye?

6 In the old rhyme, who killed Cock Robin?

7 What is the opposite of the adjective 'patient'?

8 Who was Sherlock Holmes' faithful assistant?

9 What is the past tense of the word creep?

10 What do the initials MP stand for?

ANSWERS

1. *Harry Potter and the Chamber of Secrets* 2. Spike Milligan 3. Old
4. Cookery 5. Pupil 6. The sparrow 7. Impatient 8. Doctor Watson 9. Crept
10. Member of Parliament and Military Police

QUIZ 61

• •

1 Which writer and playwright wrote *The Importance of Being Earnest* and *The Ballad of Reading Gaol*?

2 Which Harriet wrote *Uncle Tom's Cabin*?

3 Whose first novel was *Carrie*, published in 1974?

4 Who wrote *Sophie's World*?

5 Which Brontë wrote *Jane Eyre*: Charlotte, Emily or Anne?

6 Which word, meaning a bad smell, rhymes with pink?

7 Who wrote about the BFG (Big Friendly Giant)?

8 What do the initials ASAP stand for?

9 What word can mean an aircraft and a woodworking tool?

10 What word is used to describe a group of ants?

ANSWERS

1. Oscar Wilde 2. Harriet Beecher Stowe 3. Stephen King 4. Jostein Gaarder
5. Charlotte 6. Stink 7. Roald Dahl 8. As Soon As Possible 9. Plane
10. A colony

QUIZ 62

• •

1   Who wrote *The Secret Garden*?

2   Who writes fantasy novels about Discworld?

3   Who wrote *On the Origin of Species*?

4   What was the book about?

5   When you add -ly to an adjective what type of word do you normally create?

6   In Greek mythology, which character's weak point was his heel?

7   Who wrote *The Cider House Rules* and *The World According to Garp*?

8   What is the meaning of the word turmoil?

9   Which member of the British royal family wrote *The Old Man of Lochnagar* in 1980?

10 Which Shakespearean character was known as the Prince of Denmark: Othello, Hamlet or King Lear?

ANSWERS

1. Frances Hodgson Burnett 2. Terry Pratchett 3. Charles Darwin 4. The theory of evolution 5. An adverb 6. Achilles 7. John Irving 8. A state of great confusion or unrest 9. Prince Charles 10. Hamlet

QUIZ 63

• •

1 How many ugly sisters did Cinderella have?

2 What is the name of the little yellow bird in the *Peanuts* cartoons?

3 What do the initials MW stand for on a radio?

4 Which book character 'robbed from the rich and gave to the poor'?

5 Did he live in Epping Forest, Sherwood Forest or the New Forest?

6 What is the past tense of the word 'eat'?

7 Who went to London to seek his fortune and eventually became lord mayor?

8 Which postman has a black-and-white cat?

9 Can you complete the book title, *The Lion, The Witch...*?

10 What is the name of the Bogeyman in the Raymond Briggs book?

ANSWERS

1. Two 2. Woodstock 3. Medium Wave 4. Robin Hood 5. Sherwood Forest
6. Ate 7. Dick Whittington 8. Postman Pat 9. *and The Wardrobe* 10. Fungus

QUIZ 64

• •

1 Who wrote the Sherlock Holmes mysteries?

2 Which ancient Greek character fell in love with himself?

3 Who wrote the books upon which the *Jaws* films were based?

4 In which comic books would you find a character called Obelisk?

5 Who writes and draws the *Kipper* stories?

6 Who wrote *The Snowman* and *Father Christmas*?

7 Who wrote *The Hitch-Hiker's Guide to the Galaxy*?

8 Who wrote *Kubla Khan* and *The Rime of the Ancient Mariner*?

9 What animals star in the book *Ring of Bright Water*?

10 Who wrote *Emma* and *Sense and Sensibility*?

ANSWERS

1. Sir Arthur Conan Doyle 2. Narcissus 3. Robert Benchley 4. The *Asterix* books 5. Mick Inkpen 6. Raymond Briggs 7. Douglas Adams 8. Samuel Taylor Coleridge 9. Otters 10. Jane Austen

QUIZ 65

• •

1 Americans call them restrooms; what do British people call this room?

2 Which sci-fi author wrote a number of books about robots, including *I, Robot*?

3 About which mystical land did CS Lewis write?

4 What are you doing if you 'burn the candle at both ends'?

5 Complete the title of the Shakespeare play *Two Gentlemen of...*?

6 What are you doing if you are 'bending over backwards'?

7 Who wrote *Kim* and the *Just So Stories*?

8 What word do Americans use for 'undertaker'?

9 What is a scene if it is 'picturesque'?

10 In which story would you find Gandalf the wizard and Smaug the dragon?

ANSWERS

1. Toilets or lavatories 2. Isaac Asimov 3. Narnia 4. Working too hard
5. *Verona* 6. Trying very hard 7. Rudyard Kipling 8. Mortician 9. Attractive and interesting 10. *The Hobbit*

QUIZ 66

. . . .

1 Americans call them restrooms; what do British people call this room?

2 Which sci-fi author wrote a number of books about robots, including I, Robot?

3 What mystical land did C.S. Lewis write about?

4 What are you doing if you "burn the candle at both ends"?

5 Complete the title of the Shakespeare play Two Gentlemen of...?

6 What are you doing if you are "bending over backwards"?

7 Who wrote Kim and the Just-So stories?

8 What word do Americans use instead of undertakers?

9 What is a scene if it is picturesque?

10 In which story would you find Gandalf the wizard and Smaug the dragon?

ANSWERS

1. Saves nine 2. Adrian Mole 3. Gulliver's Travels 4. Lilliput 5. A swan
6. Science fiction 7. Light work 8. A tiger 9. A black panther 10. Mr Hyde

QUIZ 67

• •

1   Which book about a horse did Anna Sewell write?

2   Who wrote *My Family and Other Animals*?

3   On which Greek island was most of the book set?

4   Which Arsenal supporter wrote *Fever Pitch* and *About a Boy*?

5   Which Doctor encountered a Push-me-pull-you in his travels?

6   About which Tess did Thomas Hardy write?

7   Which Australian author wrote *Misery Guts* and *Water Wings*?

8   Who wrote the *Animal Ark* series of books?

9   Who wrote *The French Lieutenant's Woman*, *The Magus* and *The Collector*?

10 Which Shakespeare play features the characters Viola, Malvolio and Sir Toby Belch?

ANSWERS

1. *Black Beauty* 2. Gerald Durrell 3. Corfu 4. Nick Hornby 5. Doctor Dolittle
6. *Tess of the d'Urbervilles* 7. Morris Gleitzman 8. Lucy Daniels 9. John Fowles
10. *Twelfth Night*

QUIZ 68

• •

1 Is a barnacle a shellfish, a type of oar or an ancient weapon?

2 Which fairytale character sold his family's cow for a handful of beans?

3 Who wrote the original *Dr Jekyll* story?

4 What do you intend doing if you want to 'turn over a new leaf'?

5 Which sci-fi author wrote *Rendezvous With Rama*, *The Sands of Mars* and *Childhood's End*?

6 If you are asked to 'shake a leg', what should you do?

7 Who wrote *Lord of the Flies*?

8 What Shakespeare play title is considered bad luck for actors to mention?

9 Which author wrote *The Crow Road* and *The Wasp Factory*?

10 What initial does he add to his name when writing sci-fi stories?

ANSWERS

QUIZ 69

1 Did Arthur Miller or Arthur Ransome write *Swallows and Amazons*?

2 What do the initials CD stand for?

3 In which books would you find Captain Haddock and a dog called Snowy?

4 In which books would you find Linus, Lucy and Peppermint Patty?

5 Complete the title of the Shakespeare play *The Taming of...*?

6 How many days did it take for Phileas Fogg to travel around the Earth?

7 How many people would you find in a duet?

8 According to the proverb, what do 'too many cooks' do?

9 Which F word do Americans use for autumn?

10 In which tales would you find Friar Tuck and Maid Marian?

ANSWERS

1. Arthur Ransome 2. Compact Disc 3. *Tin-Tin* 4. *Peanuts* 5. *the Shrew*
6. 80 days 7. Two 8. Spoil the broth 9. Fall 10. Robin Hood

QUIZ 70

• •

1 Who wrote the *Adrian Mole* books?

2 Who was Adrian Mole's girlfriend?

3 Who wrote *Robinson Crusoe*?

4 Which Thomas wrote *The Mayor of Casterbridge* and *Jude the Obscure*?

5 Complete the title of the Shakespeare play *A Midsummer…*?

6 Does a prologue start or end a story?

7 What would be your *alma mater*?

8 Who wrote *The Time Machine* and *War of the Worlds*?

9 What word means both attractive and quite?

10 How many people would you find in a quintet?

ANSWERS

1. Sue Townsend 2. Pandora 3. Daniel Defoe 4. Thomas Hardy 5. *Night's Dream* 6. Start 7. Your old school or university 8. HG Wells 9. Pretty
10. Five

QUIZ 71

● ●

1 *Prince Caspian* and *The Voyage of the Dawn Treader* are part of which Chronicles?

2 What would you be if you were a 'stick in the mud'?

3 Which golden prize were Jason and the Argonauts seeking?

4 Is the Jason and the Argonauts story a part of ancient Greek, Roman or Viking mythology?

5 What do Americans call 'spanners'?

6 Who wrote *2001: A Space Odyssey* and had a TV series about the Mysterious World?

7 In which book do Wendy Darling and the 'lost boys' appear?

8 Which Sir Walter wrote romantic adventures including *Ivanhoe* and *Waverley*?

9 Can you complete the book title *The Last of the…*?

10 What do the initials RAC stand for?

ANSWERS

1. The Narnia Chronicles 2. Resistant to change 3. The golden fleece
4. Ancient Greek 5. Wrenches 6. Arthur C Clarke 7. *Peter Pan* 8. Sir Walter
Scott 9. *Mohicans* 10. Royal Automobile Club

QUIZ 72

• •

1   In which pantomime does Widow Twankey appear?

2   What handy aid to spelling was first compiled by Dr Samuel Johnson?

3   What is the meaning of the initials UFO?

4   Who was the one-legged pirate in the adventure story *Treasure Island*?

5   Which word is a common writing instrument and a fenced-in area to hold sheep?

6   Which American word is used to mean a lift?

7   What would you do if you 'spilled the beans'?

8   Which letter would you add to 'rain' to mean a railway vehicle?

9   Complete the title of the Shakespeare play *Anthony and…*?

10 What is the name of the lion in the Narnia books: Alvera, Leo, Aslan or Larry?

ANSWERS

QUIZ 73

• •

1 Which dramatist wrote *Pygmalion* and Arms and the Man?

2 About what sport does Dick Francis write?

3 Which children's book character lives in Nutwood?

4 Who wrote *Brideshead Revisited*, *Scoop* and *Decline and Fall*?

5 What is the surname of father and son, Kingsley and Martin, who are both writers?

6 Which novel, about a large white whale, was written by Herman Melville?

7 Which book of facts and statistics, published annually, is known as the bible of the cricket buff?

8 In which book is General Woundwort defeated by Hazel, Bigwig and Fiver?

9 Who wrote the books, adapted into television programmes, about Inspector Morse?

10 In which city did Inspector Morse work?

ANSWERS

QUIZ 74

1 Who wrote spy stories featuring the character George Smiley?

2 In which George Orwell book does Winston Smith and Room 101 appear?

3 Mary Ann Evans wrote *The Mill on the Floss* and *Middlemarch* under what name?

4 Which Irish writer wrote *Ulysses*, *Dubliners* and *A Portrait of the Artist as a Young Man*?

5 Who wrote *Tale of Two Cities*, *Martin Chuzzlewit* and *The Old Curiosity Shop*?

6 Who wrote *Peter Pan*?

7 Which humorous author wrote *Wilt*, *Blott on the Landscape* and *Porterhouse Blue*?

8 Who, according to the Bible, was the oldest man who ever lived?

9 Who wrote *To Kill a Mockingbird*?

10 Which romantic poet wrote about butterflies and daffodils?

ANSWERS

1. John Le Carré 2. 1984 3. George Eliot 4. James Joyce 5. Charles Dickens
6. JM Barrie 7. Tom Sharpe 8. Methuselah 9. Harper Lee
10. William Wordsworth

QUIZ 75

• •

1 How many bags of wool did Baa-baa Black Sheep have in the nursery rhyme?

2 Who was the leader of the Wombles?

3 Which child in the old poem is 'full of grace'?

4 Which civil war is the setting for Ernest Hemmingway's *For Whom the Bell Tolls*?

5 What word means an elevator and to raise something?

6 In which Shakespeare play would you have found Yorick: *Hamlet*, *Macbeth* or *King Lear*?

7 Which former Conservative politician wrote *The Fourth Estate* and *First Amongst Equals*?

8 What was the name of the girl who met the Mad Hatter and the Queen of Hearts?

9 What was the name of the sword in the *Tales of King Arthur*?

10 In which fairytale did a girl eat the porridge of the three bears?

ANSWERS

1. Three bags 2. Great Uncle Bulgaria 3. Tuesday's child 4. The Spanish Civil War 5. Lift 6. *Hamlet* 7. Jeffrey Archer 8. Alice 9. Excalibur 10. *Goldilocks*

QUIZ 76

• •

1   In which country are the famous pyramids of the pharaohs situated?

2   What is the capital city of Eire (Republic of Ireland)?

3   In which American city is the Empire State Building?

4   Which European country is famous for its beaches and its bull fights?

5   How many states are there in the United States?

6   Which country's cities include Yokohama and Kyoto?

7   What is the name of the continent that includes the countries Chile and Peru?

8   Is cartography the study of oceans, volcano watching or map making?

9   What type of geological feature are Australia, Malta and Iceland?

10 Which country's flag features a red maple leaf?

ANSWERS

1. Egypt 2. Dublin 3. New York 4. Spain 5. 50 6. Japan 7. South America
8. Map making 9. They are all islands 10. Canada

QUIZ 77

• •

1 What is the capital city of Australia?

2 Which European country's flag is a white cross on a red background?

3 What is the name of the second highest mountain in the world?

4 At 110 metres, what is Glomach the highest example of in Britain?

5 Which London Underground line is coloured bright red on the map?

6 Is Auckland in New Zealand's North or South Island?

7 In which country would you find the city of Cape Town?

8 What is 4,000 metres long and is near Hull?

9 Is the answer to question eight the largest of its kind in Great Britain?

10 If you were driving across the Golden Gate bridge, which city would you be in?

ANSWERS

1. Canberra 2. Switzerland 3. K2 4. Waterfall 5. Central Line 6. North
7. South Africa 8. The Humber Bridge 9. Yes. 10. San Francisco

QUIZ 78

1 What is the currency of Cyprus?

2 What is a tributary?

3 Which river, first discovered by Christopher Columbus, runs through Venezuela?

4 Which country owns Easter Island?

5 Which state in the USA has its capital based at Tallahassee?

6 With which country would you associate eating vine leaves and drinking retsina?

7 Which E word describes an exploding volcano?

8 What tiny state, just 453 square kilometres in size, is bordered by France and Spain?

9 What is the capital city of Switzerland?

10 At 5,895 metres high, what is the name of the highest mountain in Africa?

ANSWERS

1. The Cypriot pound 2. A stream that runs into a larger river 3. Orinoco 4. Chile 5. Florida 6. Greece 7. Eruption 8. Andorra 9. Bern 10. Mount Kilimanjaro

QUIZ 79

1 Where would you find stalactites and stalagmites?

2 Does a stalactite grow up or down?

3 Which competition was won by a song called Wild Dances, in 2004?

4 If a person was Dutch, which country would they come from?

5 Which stretch of sea separates England and France?

6 Which is Britain's longest river?

7 How many toes does an ostrich have on one foot?

8 What type of weather feature are cirrus and nimbus?

9 Which London transport system features the Piccadilly and Northern Lines?

10 What is the capital of Italy?

ANSWERS

1. In caves 2. Down 3. The Eurovision Song Contest 4. The Netherlands
5. The English Channel 6. River Thames 7. Two 8. Clouds 9. London
Underground 10. Rome

QUIZ 80

. . . .

1 In which continent are Brunei and Laos?

2 Which sign of the zodiac is represented by a lion?

3 Before the euro, which country's currency was the drachma?

4 Which group of islands include Sark and Alderney?

5 Which European country does the River Ebro run through?

6 In which English county are the towns of Deal and Ramsgate?

7 What is the capital of Thailand?

8 Which African country has the largest population?

9 Which sea separates Australia and New Zealand?

10 Which stretch of water separates the Isle of Wight from mainland England?

ANSWERS

1. Asia 2. Leo 3. Greece 4. The Channel Islands 5. Spain 6. Kent
7. Bangkok 8. Nigeria 9. The Tasman Sea 10. The Solent

QUIZ 81

. . . .

1 What term describes a volcano that has not been active for a time?

2 Which English city is situated on the River Mersey?

3 Which continent includes Tonga, Fiji and New Zealand?

4 What is the capital of Turkey?

5 What is Turkey's most famous city?

6 What is the largest lake in North America?

7 What is the longest river in the world?

8 Is the Australian state of Tasmania an island?

9 Of which country is Budapest the capital city?

10 What is Russia's national airline called?

ANSWERS

1. Dormant 2. Liverpool 3. Oceania 4. Ankara 5. Istanbul 6. Lake Superior
7. The Nile 8. Yes 9. Hungary 10. Aeroflot

QUIZ 82

● ●

1   In which English county does Southampton lie?
2   What country lies directly west of Spain?
3   Before the euro, what was the currency of Italy?
4   In which country would you find the Taj Mahal?
5   Which Scottish lake is allegedly home to Nessie?
6   What is the most populated city in Australia?
7   Where would you find the Eiffel Tower?
8   What is the United Kingdom's national airline?
9   Of what country is Washington DC the capital?
10 What important aid to navigation was invented
    by the Chinese 1,000 years ago?

ANSWERS

1. Hampshire 2. Portugal 3. Lire 4. India 5. Loch Ness 6. Sydney 7. Paris,
France 8. British Airways 9. The United States 10. The magnetic compass

QUIZ 83

. . . .

1 Which Scottish city has the Royal Mile, not far from Waverley station?

2 What major airport, Europe's busiest, is west of the centre of London?

3 In which country would you find organised farms called kibbutzim?

4 Which island has a capital called Valletta?

5 Which Australian state has Brisbane as its capital?

6 What is the smallest country in Europe?

7 What river, at 3,688 kilometres long, is Europe's longest?

8 What is the capital of the Philippines?

9 What is a tsunami?

10 Which continent contains the Amazon River?

ANSWERS

1. Edinburgh 2. Heathrow 3. Israel 4. Malta 5. Queensland 6. Vatican City
7. The Volga 8. Manila 9. A tidal wave 10. South America

QUIZ 84

1 Which two English cities does the Grand Union Canal link?

2 How long is the Grand Union Canal?

3 What is the smallest sovereign country in Oceania?

4 Which two Mediterranean islands are separated by the Straits of Bonifacio?

5 Which English city, apart from London, has Victoria and Piccadilly stations?

6 What is the third largest ocean?

7 What is the capital of Jersey?

8 What covers about one tenth of all land on Earth at any given time?

9 Which collection of 68 islands is also a Scottish county?

10 What type of cloud is towering, dark grey at its base and often gives heavy showers?

ANSWERS

1. Liverpool and Manchester 2. 480 kilometres 3. Nauru 4. Corsica and Sardinia 5. Manchester 6. Indian 7. St Helier 8. Ice 9. Orkney
10. Cumulonimbus

QUIZ 85

• •

1 Which is the largest continent in the world?

2 If a person was Peruvian, which country would they come from?

3 In which city would you find Marble Arch and Trafalgar Square?

4 Which three colours appear on the French flag?

5 Before the euro, which country's currency is the Deutsch Mark?

6 What is a glacier?

7 In which continent is the world's largest glacier?

8 The largest gorge in the world is in the United States. What is its name?

9 Of which geographical feature are the Kalahari and the Atacama examples?

10 Where does the Massif Central lie: in France, Austria or Switzerland?

ANSWERS

1. Asia 2. Peru 3. London 4. Blue, white and red 5. Germany 6. A huge mass of ice that flows down a mountain valley 7. Antarctica 8. The Grand Canyon 9. Deserts 10. France

QUIZ 86

1 Is Manchester Airport north, west or south of the city?

2 What is the largest town in the English county of Somerset?

3 If you got out of the London Underground at Hatton Cross, on which line would you have been travelling?

4 In which American city would you find The White House and the Smithsonian Museum?

5 What is the national airline of Spain?

6 In which English county is Stonehenge?

7 Where is the Millennium Stadium in Wales?

8 What is the capital of China?

9 What was its former name?

10 In which US state is Hollywood?

ANSWERS

1. South 2. Taunton 3. Piccadilly 4. Washington DC 5. Iberia 6. Wiltshire
7. Cardiff 8. Beijing 9. Peking 10. California

QUIZ 87

1 How many states are there in Australia?

2 Which country has more cattle than any other?

3 What is the capital of Iceland?

4 If you were in Cuzco visiting the sites of the Incas, in which country would you be?

5 What name is frequently given to Northern Ireland?

6 In which English county is Corfe Castle?

7 What is the smallest sovereign country in the continent of Africa?

8 Where is Linz?

9 Which British lake has an area of 396 square kilometres?

10 Which African country's capital city is called Lusaka?

ANSWERS

1. Eight 2. India 3. Reykjavik 4. Peru 5. Ulster 6. Dorset 7. Seychelles
8. Austria 9. Lough Neath 10. Zambia

QUIZ 88

- -

1 Where is Mount Snowdon?

2 Which two countries does Hadrian's Wall separate?

3 If you were at King's Cross railway station in London, would you be getting on a train that heads north, south or east?

4 What is the capital of Spain?

5 In which ocean are the islands of Hawaii situated?

6 Which Scottish city is famous for its summer festival of the arts?

7 Which country's flag is a red circle on a white background?

8 In which country are the indigenous people called Maoris?

9 In which country is Euro-Disney situated?

10 Which American city is called 'the windy city'?

ANSWERS

1. Wales 2. England and Scotland 3. North 4. Madrid 5. The Pacific
6. Edinburgh 7. Japan 8. New Zealand 9. France 10. Chicago

QUIZ 89

. . . .

1   If you were a Geordie, from which British city were you likely to come?

2   In which Australian state is the city of Melbourne situated?

3   If your plane landed at O'Hare airport, in which city would you have arrived?

4   On which motorway would you find Watford Gap services?

5   Which English county is known as the 'garden of England'?

6   What is the capital city of Peru?

7   Which two countries does Lake Geneva border?

8   Which is the world's largest city?

9   If you were taking photos in Red Square, which city would you be in?

10 In which country would you find the lacemakers of Bruges and the port of Antwerp?

ANSWERS

1. Newcastle-upon-Tyne 2. Victoria 3. Chicago 4. The M1 5. Kent 6. Lima
7. Switzerland and France 8. Tokyo 9. Moscow 10. Belgium

QUIZ 90

• •

1   Which northern Scottish city is famous for its connections with the oil industry?

2   What is the unit of currency of Argentina?

3   The area of Britain that includes Ipswich and Norwich is known by which regional name?

4   In which city are the skyscrapers the Chrysler Building and the Woolworth Building?

5   Where does the Grimaldi family rule?

6   What are the Quantocks?

7   Where is the southernmost tip of Great Britain?

8   What are the counties of Cornwall, Devon, Somerset and Dorset sometimes known as?

9   What does the Beaufort scale measure?

10 On the Beaufort scale, what is 12 an example of?

ANSWERS

1. Aberdeen 2. Peso 3. East Anglia 4. New York 5. Monaco 6. A range of hills 7. Land's End 8. The West Country or Wessex 9. Wind speed
10. A hurricane

QUIZ 91

. . . .

1 Ibiza is a popular holiday island in the Mediterranean Sea. Which country owns it?

2 From which country do Aboriginals come?

3 In which ocean would you find Fiji and Papua New Guinea?

4 Where would you find the Louvre museum, which houses the Mona Lisa painting?

5 In which city would you be if you were standing on the harbour bridge looking at the opera house?

6 What is the name of Homer Simpson's youngest child?

7 In which country would you find the Great Wall?

8 If you went on holiday in Provence or the Dordogne, in which country would you be?

9 Which English county includes the towns Penzance, St Ives and Truro?

10 From London, in which direction does the M4 take drivers?

ANSWERS

1. Spain 2. Australia 3. Pacific 4. Paris, France 5. Sydney, Australia 6. Maggie
7. China 8. France 9. Cornwall 10. West

QUIZ 92

. . . .

1 Which motorway ring road circles Manchester?

2 Which country in the British Isles features the highest point?

3 When molten rock is forced upwards, cools and becomes solid, what is it called?

4 Which long wooden tube do Aboriginals use to make music?

5 Which country's currency is the yen?

6 What is the largest volcano in the world?

7 In which group of islands can it be found?

8 In which country is the Muslim holy city of Mecca?

9 If your plane landed at Orly airport, in which city would you have arrived?

10 Which country's population is estimated at 1.4 billion?

ANSWERS

1. M60 2. Scotland (Ben Nevis) 3. Igneous 4. Didgeridoo 5. Japan
6. Mauna Loa 7. The Hawaiian Islands 8. Saudi Arabia 9. Paris, France
10. China

QUIZ 93

1 Which large island lies to the east of Mozambique in Africa?

2 What is the largest country in Africa?

3 What was the country of Zimbabwe formerly called?

4 What is the longest river in the Indian subcontinent?

5 What is the capital city of Ecuador?

6 What covers just 6 percent of the Earth's surface yet contains 75 percent of all known species of plants and animals?

7 What is the capital of the Ukraine?

8 What does an anemometer measure?

9 In which country is Mount McKinley the highest peak?

10 Which Eastern European country's currency is the zloty?

ANSWERS

1. Madagascar 2. Sudan 3. Rhodesia 4. The Indus 5. Quito 6. Amazonian Rainforest 7. Kiev 8. Wind speed 9. United States 10. Poland

QUIZ 94

1 Which continent has 17,700 kilometres of coastline and includes the features Vinson Massif and Ross Island?

2 In which country would you find the Black Forest?

3 Which country is sandwiched between France and the Netherlands?

4 What is that country's capital city?

5 Which Scandinavian country's flag is a yellow cross on a blue background?

6 What is the national airline of Germany?

7 What currency do Canadians use?

8 If land is called agricultural, what is it used for?

9 What is measured in centigrade?

10 Which country's flag is known as the star-spangled banner?

ANSWERS

1. Antarctica 2. Germany 3. Belgium 4. Brussels 5. Sweden 6. Lufthansa
7. Canadian dollar 8. Farming 9. Temperature 10. The United States

QUIZ 95

• •

1   Which country has Zagreb as its capital?

2   What claim to fame does the desert area of
    Atacama have?

3   In which country is the Atacama desert?

4   Which lake is situated in the middle of Hyde Park
    in London?

5   What types of rock are sandstone and limestone?

6   How thick is the South Pole ice cap: 50 metres,
    150 metres or 1,500 metres?

7   Which canal connects the Mediterranean Sea to
    the Red Sea?

8   Through which country does it run?

9   Of what is demography the study?

10 Which three colours make up the Italian flag?

ANSWERS

1. Croatia 2. The driest place on Earth 3. Chile 4. The Serpentine
5. Sedimentary 6. 1,500 metres 7. The Suez canal 8. Egypt 9. Populations
10. Green, white and red

QUIZ 96

1 Which country has 19 major languages and includes the cities of Bangalore and Kanpur?

2 What is the capital of Sri Lanka?

3 Which is the smallest US state?

4 Which country was formerly called Siam?

5 On which river does the Canadian city of Quebec stand?

6 In which country would you find the city of Kathmandu?

7 Which country's capital city is Phnom Penh?

8 What is a tor?

9 What term means the ocean surface?

10 Which South American country's capital city is Bogotá?

ANSWERS

1. India 2. Colombo 3. Rhode Island 4. Thailand 5. St Lawrence 6. Nepal
7. Cambodia 8. A mass of rock on top of a hill 9. Sea level 10. Colombia

QUIZ 97

. . . .

1. In which country would you be if you were on the beaches of Benidorm or the Costa del Sol?

2. Off which country's coast is the island of Anglesey?

3. Which is the largest country in North America?

4. What is the capital of Portugal?

5. There are two official languages of Belgium; one is Flemish, what is the other?

6. Which continent has the most people?

7. Which Scandinavian country's capital city is Helsinki?

8. Which city in Europe has the biggest population: Paris, London or Bonn?

9. In which continent has the lowest-ever temperature on Earth been recorded?

10. Was that temperature –45 degrees, –90 degrees or –180 degrees centigrade?

ANSWERS

1. Spain 2. Wales 3. Canada 4. Lisbon 5. French 6. Asia 7. Finland
8. London 9. Antarctica 10. –90 degrees

QUIZ 98

. . . .

1 In which country is the rainiest place on Earth?

2 How much rain does this place receive every year;
   1,500, 2,000 or 11,000 millimetres?

3 Which American state has two coastlines – one
   facing the Atlantic Ocean and the other facing
   the Gulf of Mexico?

4 What does a barometer measure?

5 Which map scale would offer you more detail:
   1:50,000 or 1:500?

6 Is London or Sheffield closer to Birmingham?

7 Which stretch of water does the city of Edinburgh
   overlook?

8 Which is the smallest of the world's four oceans?

9 What name do we give to a natural hot water
   fountain?

10 In which English county would you find the
   national park of Dartmoor?

ANSWERS

1. Bangladesh 2. 11,000 millimetres 3. Florida 4. Atmospheric pressure
5. 1:500 6. Sheffield 7. Firth of Forth 8. Arctic Ocean 9. Geyser 10. Devon

QUIZ 99

1 What colour flag is flown on a beach declared clean and free of avoidable pollution?

2 Which Welsh county contains Newport and Pontypool?

3 Of what are there 535 active versions on Earth, 80 of them underwater?

4 Which Asian country has the capital city of Ulan Bator?

5 What is the name of the world's highest navigable lake?

6 Which two countries does it span?

7 In which continent would you be if you were on the island of Kiribati?

8 What is a fjord?

9 Which country's capital city is Kabul?

10 In which country would you find the holiday resort of Eilat?

ANSWERS

1. Blue 2. Gwent 3. Volcanoes 4. Mongolia 5. Lake Titicaca 6. Peru and Bolivia 7. Oceania 8. A long, narrow, coastal inlet 9. Afghanistan 10. Israel

QUIZ 100

1 Which country has the bullet train?

2 What is the name of the world's biggest desert, which covers much of North Africa?

3 Discounting Australia, what is the largest island in the world?

4 In which continent do Masai and Zulu people live?

5 Which E word describes the process of rocks being worn away?

6 Which French and British towns offer the shortest route between the two countries?

7 In which country would you find Uluru (formerly Ayers Rock)?

8 Where do Sherpa people live: Siberia, Nepal or Malaysia?

9 Which country's national airline is KLM?

10 In which city would you find Times Square and Manhattan?

ANSWERS

1. Japan 2. Sahara Desert 3. Greenland 4. Africa 5. Erosion 6. Calais and Dover 7. Australia 8. Nepal 9. The Netherlands 10. New York

QUIZ 101

• •

1   What is the imaginary circle drawn around the world the same distance from both poles?

2   JAL is the national airline of which country?

3   What is the largest state in the United States?

4   What is the name of the highest waterfall in the world?

5   Which islands are found in the South Atlantic and still have their ownership disputed?

6   Which two countries lay claim to owning these islands?

7   Was the largest recorded iceberg bigger or smaller than Belgium?

8   Which island has the capital of Douglas?

9   In which sea would you find the above island?

10 In which continent would you find Niagara Falls?

ANSWERS

1. The Equator 2. Japan 3. Alaska 4. Angel Falls 5. The Falklands
6. Argentina and Britain 7. Bigger 8. Isle of Man 9. Irish Sea 10. North America

QUIZ 102

• •

1 What holds about 230,000 cubic kilometres of water?

2 Which is the highest mountain in Oceania?

3 In which country is it situated?

4 Which language do most people speak in Guatemala?

5 What is the capital city of Bulgaria?

6 What is Canada's smallest province?

7 Which is the second largest desert in the world?

8 Is Zambia in the Northern or Southern Hemisphere?

9 What killed 45,000 people in northern Armenia in 1988?

10 What is the largest lake in Africa?

ANSWERS

1. The world's rivers 2. Mount Wilhelm 3. Papua New Guinea 4. Spanish
5. Sofia 6. Prince Edward Island 7. The Australian desert 8. Southern
9. An earthquake 10. Lake Victoria

QUIZ 103

• •

1   In which country would you find the town of Pisa?

2   Which is Pisa's most famous building?

3   Which English county neighbours Cornwall?

4   What is the capital of Norway?

5   Before the euro, which country's currency was the peseta?

6   Which country's capital city is Brasilia?

7   Which ocean separates Europe and North America?

8   In which continent would you find the Alps?

9   What are the Alps?

10 What is the name of the very hot fluid that comes out of a volcano?

ANSWERS

1. Italy 2. The Leaning Tower 3. Devon 4. Oslo 5. Spain 6. Brazil
7. The Atlantic 8. Europe 9. A mountain range 10. Lava

QUIZ 104

1 Which Asian country's currency is the baht?

2 What sort of boat is found on the canals of Venice?

3 What is notable about the Mariana Trench?

4 In which body of water can it be found?

5 What does the 'DC' in Washington DC stand for?

6 Which sea separates Greece from Turkey?

7 What is the name of the wandering people of the Arabian deserts?

8 Which river flows through the cities of Bonn and Cologne?

9 In which Australian state is the town of Hobart?

10 In which country is Damascus?

ANSWERS

1. Thailand 2. Gondola 3. It is the deepest part of the ocean yet found
4. Pacific Ocean 5. District of Columbia 6. Aegean 7. Bedouin 8. The Rhine
9. Tasmania 10. Syria

QUIZ 105

1 On which ocean does the coast of Tanzania lie?

2 Before the euro, which European country's currency was the escudo?

3 In what part of Britain would you be if you were walking alongside Lake Windermere?

4 Which mountain chain runs from north to south through much of South America's length?

5 What is a typhoon?

6 On which island is the volcano Mount Etna?

7 Which two European countries does the Gulf of Bothnia separate?

8 How many of the world's highest mountains are found in Asia: 7, 17 or 67?

9 In which English county are the Mendip Hills situated?

10 Which country's capital city is Islamabad?

ANSWERS

1. Indian Ocean 2. Portugal 3. The Lake District 4. The Andes 5. A violent hurricane 6. Sicily 7. Finland and Sweden 8. 67 9. Somerset 10. Pakistan

QUIZ 106

• •

1 What type of weather is drizzle?

2 Which three colours are found on the flag of Belgium?

3 What do Perth, Darwin and Adelaide all have in common?

4 What is the capital of Mexico?

5 In which country might you eat feta cheese after visiting the Parthenon?

6 Which European country's currency is the schilling?

7 What is a low place in between hills called?

8 Which river flows through the city of Paris?

9 Does the island of Corsica belong to France or Italy?

10 In which country might you eat bird's nest soup after visiting Shanghai?

ANSWERS

1. Very light rain 2. Black, yellow and red 3. They are all Australian cities
4. Mexico City 5. Greece 6. Austria 7. A valley 8. The Seine 9. France
10. China

QUIZ 107

1 In which English county would you find Blackpool?

2 Which city is situated on the River Clyde?

3 From what product does Kuwait derive most of its income?

4 What is the capital of Denmark?

5 Which mountains divide France and Spain?

6 Which is the largest country in the Middle East?

7 In which city are there more canals: Venice or Birmingham?

8 Which US state is directly north of California?

9 What is the Matterhorn?

10 In which country is the port of Antwerp?

ANSWERS

1. Lancashire 2. Glasgow 3. Oil 4. Copenhagen 5. The Pyrenees 6. Saudi Arabia 7. Birmingham 8. Oregon 9. A mountain in the Alps 10. Belgium

QUIZ 108

• •

1 What is measured on the Richter scale?

2 Which is the largest of the Australian states?

3 What is the term used to describe the cooling effect of wind on the skin?

4 Which South American country's name means 'land of silver'?

5 What are antipodes?

6 Which German city was divided by a wall for nearly forty years?

7 Where in England would you find the Golden Mile?

8 Which Asian country, with the capital city of Jakarta, has over 170 million inhabitants?

9 In which place in Britain would you find the Bull Ring and New Street railway station?

10 Which is the longest river in Asia?

ANSWERS

1. Earthquakes 2. Western Australia 3. Wind chill 4. Argentina 5. Two places on opposite sides of the Earth 6. Berlin 7. Blackpool 8. Indonesia
9. Birmingham 10. Yangtzee (Chang Jiang) river in China

QUIZ 109

• •

1   If you were travelling from Los Angeles to visit Disneyland, which American state would you be in?

2   Which country produces more coffee than any other?

3   Antrim, Armagh and Londonderry are in which part of the United Kingdom?

4   What is the capital of Wales?

5   Inside which Italian city is the Vatican City situated?

6   Which continent is one and a half times bigger than the United States?

7   Through how many African countries does the Equator pass: two, six or thirteen?

8   If you were cycling through Amsterdam, which country would you be visiting?

9   Which US state includes the city of Dallas and is known as the 'Lone Star' state?

10   In which country is the region of Normandy?

ANSWERS

1. California 2. Brazil 3. Northern Ireland 4. Cardiff 5. Rome 6. Antarctica
7. Six 8. The Netherlands 9. Texas 10. France

QUIZ 110

1 Which feature of Earth's oceans does the Moon affect?

2 What is the most common language spoken on Earth?

3 In which ocean is the island of Tahiti?

4 What is the capital of Malaysia?

5 Which country's national airline is Varig?

6 From north to south, which is the world's longest country?

7 In which country would you be if you were travelling from Marrakesh to Fès?

8 In which country is the world's coldest city?

9 What does a seismograph measure?

10 In which country, beginning with the letter M, is Timbuktu situated?

ANSWERS

1. The tides 2. Mandarin 3. Pacific Ocean 4. Kuala Lumpur 5. Brazil 6. Chile
7. Morocco 8. Mongolia 9. Earthquakes 10. Mali

QUIZ 111

. . . .

1 Which region of the Arctic includes parts of Norway, Russia, Sweden and Finland?

2 What is the measurement and mapping of the Earth called?

3 Which country has four times as many pigs as any other nation?

4 In which country is the world's second-highest mountain situated?

5 Where is the Ross Ice Shelf?

6 Which African country is the most popular safari destination in the world?

7 What gruesome name is given to the United States' hottest place?

8 In which sea would you find St Lucia, Trinidad and Tobago?

9 What is the capital of Zimbabwe?

10 If you were admiring St Basil's Cathedral, in which capital city would you be?

ANSWERS

1. Lapland 2. Surveying 3. China 4. Pakistan 5. Antarctica 6. Kenya
7. Death Valley 8. The Caribbean 9. Harare 10. Moscow

QUIZ 112

. . . .

1 What is known as London's third airport?

2 In which part of London is the Millennium Dome situated?

3 Which London Underground line's most northern station is Walthamstow?

4 What is a monsoon?

5 Which country is bordered by China and Russia?

6 Which North African country has the capital city of Tripoli?

7 Which country is the world's leading coal producer?

8 From what country did Christopher Columbus set sail?

9 In which ocean is the world's deepest underwater trench?

10 In which country is Shensi Province?

ANSWERS

1. Stansted 2. Greenwich 3. Victoria line 4. A wind that brings heavy rains
5. Mongolia 6. Libya 7. USA 8. Spain 9. Pacific Ocean 10. China

QUIZ 113

1 What is the real name of the singer formerly known as Ginger Spice?

2 How many points is the bulls-eye worth in darts?

3 What is the name of the spaceman in *Toy Story 2*?

4 In which TV show would you find characters called Marg and Homer?

5 What is a hundred runs called in cricket?

6 What is the name of the teenage witch who lives with her aunts and a talking cat?

7 Which football team plays at White Hart Lane?

8 Which films featured terrifying creatures called Raptors?

9 Which football team didn't enter the 1999/2000 FA Cup?

10 Where would you find a hoop, a backboard and a three point line?

ANSWERS

1. Geri Halliwell 2. 50 3. Buzz Lightyear 4. *The Simpsons* 5. A century
6. Sabrina 7. Tottenham Hotspur 8. *Jurassic Park* 9. Manchester United
10. A basketball court

QUIZ 114

. . . .

1 Which football club has Elton John as its chairman?

2 Which town do the Flintstones come from?

3 Which famous boxer was voted sportsperson of the millennium?

4 Which famous singer was co-manager of the boyband Westlife?

5 Which Formula One team is managed by Ron Dennis?

6 Which famous Australian fast bowler once tried to use an aluminium bat?

7 What is the most expensive property on a Monopoly board?

8 How many points are given for a rugby union drop goal?

9 Which football team has the nickname The Owls?

10 Which comic actor played Fletcher in *Porridge* and Arkwright in *Open All Hours*?

ANSWERS

1. Watford 2. Bedrock 3. Muhammad Ali 4. Ronan Keating 5. McClaren
6. Dennis Lillee 7. Mayfair 8. Three 9. Sheffield Wednesday 10. Ronnie
Barker

QUIZ 115

1. Westlife's single 'I Had A Dream' was performed in the 1970s by which band?

2. Which space is diagonally opposite 'Go' on a Monopoly board?

3. How many grand slam tournaments are there in tennis?

4. Which successful Scottish football club did Sir Alex Ferguson manage before Manchester United?

5. Kobe Bryant, Magic Johnson and Wilt Chamberlain all played which sport?

6. What is the first word of the Lord's Prayer?

7. If you had a mashie and a niblick in your bag, what sport would you be playing?

8. Which TV show features the characters Xander, Willow and Angel?

9. Which national cricket team featured the talented Crowe brothers?

10. Which rugby league club plays at the JJB Stadium?

ANSWERS

1. Abba 2. Free parking 3. Four 4. Aberdeen 5. Basketball 6. Our 7. Golf
8. *Buffy the Vampire Slayer* 9. New Zealand 10. Wigan

QUIZ 116

• •

1 How many pockets are there on a snooker table?

2 Which football team play at Elland Road?

3 Which American TV show featured three pairs of flat-sharing pals?

4 Which actor/rapper recorded an album called 'Willennium'?

5 Which sport did *Gladiators* presenter John Fashanu once play professionally?

6 What nationality is the band Catatonia?

7 Which nation's rugby team are known as the All Blacks?

8 What was the title of Westlife's debut album?

9 For which country does batsman Sachin Tendulkar play?

10 Which TV show featured Laurence, Carol and Handy Andy?

ANSWERS

1. Six 2. Leeds United 3. *Friends* 4. Will Smith 5. Football 6. Welsh 7. New Zealand 8. *Westlife* 9. India 10. *Changing Rooms*

QUIZ 117

1 Which British rower gained a world record number of Olympic gold medals?

2 Which TV show featured a radio psychiatrist who lives with his father, a pet dog and a home help?

3 Which former England cricket captain went on to be team captain on a comedy quiz show?

4 Which county did he play cricket for?

5 In which song do six geese follow five golden rings?

6 How many players are in an Australian Rules team: 12, 15 or 18?

7 In which band did Bill Wyman play for over twenty years?

8 Richard Dunwoody is a leading participant in which sport?

9 What leisure pursuit comes in coarse, fly and sea forms?

10 Which fez-wearing comedian had the catchphrase 'just like that'?

ANSWERS

1. Steve Redgrave 2. *Frasier* 3. David Gower 4. Leicestershire
5. The 12 Days of Christmas 6. 18 7. The Rolling Stones 8. Horse-racing
9. Fishing 10. Tommy Cooper

QUIZ 118

. . . .

1   Who finished second in the 1999 Formula One Championship?

2   Whose 1999 album was entitled 'Come On Over'?

3   Which British tennis player was beaten by Chris Woodruff in the 2000 Australian Open?

4   In golf, what is a hole completed in one under par called?

5   Which American female singer starred in the film *The Bodyguard*?

6   Who hosted the show *Masterchef*?

7   Which girl band, whose hits include 'Whole Again' and 'The Tide is High', announced their break-up in 2004?

8   Who won the 1999 Football League Cup?

9   Which film actress was married to Tom Cruise?

10 Who did Manchester United beat in the final of the 1999 European Champions League?

ANSWERS

1. Eddie Irvine 2. Shania Twain 3. Tim Henman 4. A birdie 5. Whitney Houston 6. Loyd Grossman 7. Sport First 8. Tottenham Hotspur 9. Nicole Kidman 10. Bayern Munich

QUIZ 122

1. Is Phil Tufnell a fast or spin bowler?
2. For which football team do Kanu and Ray Parlour play?
3. What type of creature is the computer game character Sonic?
4. From which city did the Beatles originate?
5. Who was the shy dwarf in *Snow White*?
6. How many teams are relegated from the Premiership every year?
7. Which TV show features Del Boy and Rodney Trotter?
8. Which elephant could fly?
9. In what sport would you use parallel bars?
10. When were the Olympic Games held in Barcelona?

ANSWERS

1. Spin bowler 2. Arsenal 3. A hedgehog 4. Liverpool 5. Bashful 6. Three
7. *Only Fools and Horses* 8. Dumbo 9. Gymnastics 10. 1996

QUIZ 119

1. How many dalmations were there in the famous book and Disney film?
2. What nationality is fast bowler Allan Donald?
3. What was Winnie the Pooh's favourite food?
4. What sport does John Parrott, play?
5. For which country does footballer Ronaldo play?
6. Where is Britain's one tennis grand slam tournament played?
7. Pixie and Trixie starred in a cartoon with a cat: what was its name?
8. What is the name of the only Welsh county cricket team?
9. Which TV show features the characters Dot Cotton and Phil Mitchell?
10. What are Monza and Brands Hatch?

ANSWERS

1. 101 2. South African 3. Honey 4. Snooker 5. Brazil 6. Wimbledon
7. Mr Jinx 8. Glamorgan 9. *EastEnders* 10. Motor racing tracks

QUIZ 120

1 How many points is a blue ball worth in snooker?

2 If you saw three slips and a gully, among others, what sport would you be watching?

3 Which cartoon rabbit is always seen chewing carrots?

4 Which football team play at Villa Park?

5 Which action hero starred in the *Die Hard* series of films?

6 With which sport are promoters Frank Warren and Don King associated?

7 What is the name of Batman's road vehicle?

8 Which film star first shot to fame playing a disco star in *Saturday Night Fever*?

9 Who is the manager of Leeds United football club?

10 In which sport do you get three strikes before you are out?

ANSWERS

1. Five 2. Cricket 3. Bugs Bunny 4. Aston Villa 5. Bruce Willis 6. Boxing
7. The Batmobile 8. John Travolta 9. David O'Leary 10. Baseball

QUIZ 121

1 Who was the first player to hit six sixes off one over in cricket?

2 Which sport features teams of ten with up to 13 substitutes, all wearing protective helmets?

3 Can you name the teenage son in the TV show *The Royle Family*?

4 How many test cricket nations are there?

5 What was the name of the postman in the series *Cheers*?

6 Which *Toy Story* character does the same actor provide the voice for?

7 Which *Friends* character was played by actor David Schwimmer?

8 Which three events occur on the second day of a women's heptathlon?

9 In which year did Jesse Owens win four Olympic gold medals in running events and the long jump?

10 Who did Lisa Tarbuck replace on *The Big Breakfast*?

ANSWERS

1. Sir Garfield Sobers 2. Lacrosse 3. Anthony 4. Nine 5. Cliff (Claven)
6. Mr Potato Head 7. Ross 8. Long jump, javelin and 800 metres 9. 1936
10. Kelly Brook

QUIZ 123

1 For which athletics discipline was Sally Gunnell famous?

2 Who is the female host of *Ready, Steady, Cook*?

3 Where were the 1994 Olympics held?

4 What sport do the brothers Scott and Craig Quinnell play?

5 What is the name of the plastic peg used to raise the ball in golf?

6 Who plays Scully in the show *The X Files*?

7 Which football team play at Maine Road?

8 How many times a normal word score are the red squares worth on a Scrabble board?

9 Which TV soap features a mother and son called Pauline and Martin?

10 How many pieces are there on a draught or checkers board at the start?

ANSWERS

1. 400-metres hurdles 2. Fern Britten 3. Atlanta, USA 4. Rugby union
5. A tee 6. Gillian Anderson 7. Manchester City 8. Three times 9. *EastEnders*
(the Fowlers) 10. 24

QUIZ 124

- -

1 Who was named 1999 world footballer of the year by FIFA?

2 In which sport might a Fosbury Flop be performed?

3 Which rugby team play at The Stoop?

4 Which *Friends* star appeared in the movie *Lost in Space*?

5 Which French football star appears in shampoo commercials and *Stars in Their Eyes*?

6 How many players are there in a rugby league team?

7 Which is Britain's largest record company?

8 Which Scottish footballer sits alongside Gary Lineker on *Match of the Day*?

9 Where would you find The Chair and Beecher's Brook?

10 How many series of *Blackadder* were there?

ANSWERS

QUIZ 125

1 What was so amazing about the pig called Babe?

2 What weight did Frank Bruno used to box at?

3 Which doctor had a phone box for a time machine?

4 What is the name of Sunderland football club's stadium?

5 Which country won the 1998 football World Cup?

6 Who played *Blackadder* in the TV series?

7 What type of hat did Laurel and Hardy both wear?

8 For which county does batsman and wicketkeeper Alec Stewart play?

9 How many dwarves featured in the story of *Snow White*?

10 How many points is the pink ball worth in snooker?

ANSWERS

1. It could talk 2. Heavyweight 3. Dr Who 4. The Stadium of Light 5. France
6. Rowan Atkinson 7. A bowler hat 8. Surrey 9. Seven 10. Six

QUIZ 126

. . . .

1 Who is Batman's sidekick?

2 Who is the world number one in golf?

3 Which sport does Ian Botham's son, Liam, play?

4 What was the name of Fred Flintstone's next door neighbour and buddy?

5 How many holes are there on a standard golf course?

6 What type of creature was the star of *Jaws*?

7 In which decade is the comedy drama *The Grimleys* set?

8 For what country does Ryan Giggs play?

9 Which sport are Duncan Goodhew and Mark Foster associated with?

10 Which Australian entertainer hosts a show about animal hospitals?

ANSWERS

1. Robin 2. Tiger Woods 3. Rugby union 4. Barney Rubble 5. 18 6. A shark
7. The 1970s 8. Wales 9. Swimming 10. Rolf Harris

QUIZ 127

• •

1   Who played Batman in the 1989 film of the same name?

2   Which 1980s American soap opera featured Sue Ellen and Bobby?

3   Who was the manager of Chelsea football club before Gianluca Vialli?

4   Which radio station features disc jockey Terry Wogan?

5   Which glam rock singer was a star in the show *The Grimleys*?

6   Where are British Formula One races usually held?

7   Which TV personality has a brother called Paul, also a TV presenter?

8   In what sport could you perform a triple toe loop?

9   Which controversial comedy drama is set in a fictional town called Royston Vasey?

10 Who played Fred Flintstone in the live action film of the cartoon?

ANSWERS

1. Michael Keaton 2. Dallas 3. Ruud Gullit 4. Radio Two 5. Noddy Holder of Slade 6. Silverstone 7. Jonathon Ross 8. Ice skating 9. *The League of Gentlemen* 10. John Goodman

QUIZ 128

• •

1 What was the name of the big bear in *The Jungle Book*?

2 Which sports stadium had its twin towers torn down for redevelopment?

3 Which county cricket side do Darren Gough and Chris Silverwood play for?

4 What Australian TV programme occurs largely on Ramsey Street?

5 What was the name of Mickey Mouse's dog?

6 Which chess piece can only move diagonally?

7 Who is Yogi Bear's pint-sized pal?

8 Which band features Bono and The Edge?

9 What is the name of the sand-filled depressions around a golf course?

10 Which Hollywood film actress starred in *Notting Hill*?

ANSWERS

1. Baloo 2. Wembley stadium 3. Yorkshire 4. Neighbours 5. Pluto 6. The bishop 7. Boo-Boo 8. U2 9. Bunkers 10. Julia Roberts

QUIZ 119

. . . .

1 How many dalmations were there in the famous book and Disney film?

2 What nationality is fast bowler Allan Donald?

3 What was Winnie the Pooh's favourite food?

4 What sport does John Parrott, play?

5 For which country does footballer Ronaldo play?

6 Where is Britain's one tennis grand slam tournament played?

7 Pixie and Trixie starred in a cartoon with a cat: what was its name?

8 What is the name of the only Welsh county cricket team?

9 Which TV show features the characters Dot Cotton and Phil Mitchell?

10 What are Monza and Brands Hatch?

ANSWERS

1. 101 2. South African 3. Honey 4. Snooker 5. Brazil 6. Wimbledon
7. Mr Jinx 8. Glamorgan 9. *EastEnders* 10. Motor racing tracks

QUIZ 120

• •

1 How many points is a blue ball worth in snooker?

2 If you saw three slips and a gully, among others, what sport would you be watching?

3 Which cartoon rabbit is always seen chewing carrots?

4 Which football team play at Villa Park?

5 Which action hero starred in the *Die Hard* series of films?

6 With which sport are promoters Frank Warren and Don King associated?

7 What is the name of Batman's road vehicle?

8 Which film star first shot to fame playing a disco star in *Saturday Night Fever*?

9 Who is the manager of Leeds United football club?

10 In which sport do you get three strikes before you are out?

ANSWERS

1. Five 2. Cricket 3. Bugs Bunny 4. Aston Villa 5. Bruce Willis 6. Boxing
7. The Batmobile 8. John Travolta 9. David O'Leary 10. Baseball

QUIZ 121

1. Who was the first player to hit six sixes off one over in cricket?

2. Which sport features teams of ten with up to 13 substitutes, all wearing protective helmets?

3. Can you name the teenage son in the TV show *The Royle Family*?

4. How many test cricket nations are there?

5. What was the name of the postman in the series *Cheers*?

6. Which *Toy Story* character does the same actor provide the voice for?

7. Which *Friends* character was played by actor David Schwimmer?

8. Which three events occur on the second day of a women's heptathlon?

9. In which year did Jesse Owens win four Olympic gold medals in running events and the long jump?

10. Who did Lisa Tarbuck replace on *The Big Breakfast*?

ANSWERS

1. Sir Garfield Sobers 2. Lacrosse 3. Anthony 4. Nine 5. Cliff (Claven)
6. Mr Potato Head 7. Ross 8. Long jump, javelin and 800 metres 9. 1936
10. Kelly Brook

QUIZ 122

1 Is Phil Tufnell a fast or spin bowler?

2 For which football team do Kanu and Ray Parlour play?

3 What type of creature is the computer game character Sonic?

4 From which city did the Beatles originate?

5 Who was the shy dwarf in *Snow White*?

6 How many teams are relegated from the Premiership every year?

7 Which TV show features Del Boy and Rodney Trotter?

8 Which elephant could fly?

9 In what sport would you use parallel bars?

10 When were the Olympic Games held in Barcelona?

ANSWERS

1. Spin bowler 2. Arsenal 3. A hedgehog 4. Liverpool 5. Bashful 6. Three
7. *Only Fools and Horses* 8. Dumbo 9. Gymnastics 10. 1996

QUIZ 128

. . . .

1 What was the name of the big bear in *The Jungle Book*?

2 Which sports stadium had its twin towers torn down for redevelopment?

3 Which county cricket side do Darren Gough and Chris Silverwood play for?

4 What Australian TV programme occurs largely on Ramsey Street?

5 What was the name of Mickey Mouse's dog?

6 Which chess piece can only move diagonally?

7 Who is Yogi Bear's pint-sized pal?

8 Which band features Bono and The Edge?

9 What is the name of the sand-filled depressions around a golf course?

10 Which Hollywood film actress starred in *Notting Hill*?

ANSWERS

1. Baloo 2. Wembley stadium 3. Yorkshire 4. Neighbours 5. Pluto 6. The bishop 7. Boo-Boo 8. U2 9. Bunkers 10. Julia Roberts

QUIZ 127

. . . .

1 Who played Batman in the 1989 film of the same name?

2 Which 1980s American soap opera featured Sue Ellen and Bobby?

3 Who was the manager of Chelsea football club before Gianluca Vialli?

4 Which radio station features disc jockey Terry Wogan?

5 Which glam rock singer was a star in the show *The Grimleys*?

6 Where are British Formula One races usually held?

7 Which TV personality has a brother called Paul, also a TV presenter?

8 In what sport could you perform a triple toe loop?

9 Which controversial comedy drama is set in a fictional town called Royston Vasey?

10 Who played Fred Flintstone in the live action film of the cartoon?

ANSWERS

1. Michael Keaton 2. Dallas 3. Ruud Gullit 4. Radio Two 5. Noddy Holder of Slade 6. Silverstone 7. Jonathon Ross 8. Ice skating 9. *The League of Gentlemen* 10. John Goodman

QUIZ 126

• •

1 Who is Batman's sidekick?

2 Who is the world number one in golf?

3 Which sport does Ian Botham's son, Liam, play?

4 What was the name of Fred Flintstone's next door neighbour and buddy?

5 How many holes are there on a standard golf course?

6 What type of creature was the star of *Jaws*?

7 In which decade is the comedy drama *The Grimleys* set?

8 For what country does Ryan Giggs play?

9 Which sport are Duncan Goodhew and Mark Foster associated with?

10 Which Australian entertainer hosts a show about animal hospitals?

ANSWERS

1. Robin 2. Tiger Woods 3. Rugby union 4. Barney Rubble 5. 18 6. A shark
7. The 1970s 8. Wales 9. Swimming 10. Rolf Harris

QUIZ 125

1. What was so amazing about the pig called Babe?

2. What weight did Frank Bruno used to box at?

3. Which doctor had a phone box for a time machine?

4. What is the name of Sunderland football club's stadium?

5. Which country won the 1998 football World Cup?

6. Who played *Blackadder* in the TV series?

7. What type of hat did Laurel and Hardy both wear?

8. For which county does batsman and wicketkeeper Alec Stewart play?

9. How many dwarves featured in the story of *Snow White*?

10. How many points is the pink ball worth in snooker?

ANSWERS

1. It could talk 2. Heavyweight 3. Dr Who 4. The Stadium of Light 5. France
6. Rowan Atkinson 7. A bowler hat 8. Surrey 9. Seven 10. Six

QUIZ 124

● ●

1 Who was named 1999 world footballer of the year by FIFA?

2 In which sport might a Fosbury Flop be performed?

3 Which rugby team play at The Stoop?

4 Which *Friends* star appeared in the movie *Lost in Space*?

5 Which French football star appears in shampoo commercials and *Stars in Their Eyes*?

6 How many players are there in a rugby league team?

7 Which is Britain's largest record company?

8 Which Scottish footballer sits alongside Gary Lineker on *Match of the Day*?

9 Where would you find The Chair and Beecher's Brook?

10 How many series of *Blackadder* were there?

ANSWERS

1. Rivaldo 2. The High Jump 3. Harlequins 4. Matt Le Blanc (Joey in *Friends*)
5. David Ginola 6. 13 7. EMI 8. Alan Hansen 9. Aintree racecourse 10. Four

QUIZ 123

• •

1   For which athletics discipline was Sally Gunnell famous?

2   Who is the female host of *Ready, Steady, Cook*?

3   Where were the 1994 Olympics held?

4   What sport do the brothers Scott and Craig Quinnell play?

5   What is the name of the plastic peg used to raise the ball in golf?

6   Who plays Scully in the show *The X Files*?

7   Which football team play at Maine Road?

8   How many times a normal word score are the red squares worth on a Scrabble board?

9   Which TV soap features a mother and son called Pauline and Martin?

10 How many pieces are there on a draught or checkers board at the start?

ANSWERS

1. 400-metres hurdles 2. Fern Britten 3. Atlanta, USA 4. Rugby union
5. A tee 6. Gillian Anderson 7. Manchester City 8. Three times 9. *EastEnders*
(the Fowlers) 10. 24

QUIZ 129

· ·

1 What are the first names of the tennis-playing Williams sisters?

2 Which city did Batman do his best to protect?

3 Which county cricket side plays at Headingley?

4 What was Superman's ordinary name?

5 Which country of the British Isles has the thistle as its national symbol?

6 Which band was Gary Barlow in before he went solo?

7 Which American tennis player was famous for his on-court tantrums?

8 Ventriloquist Bob Carolgees had a dog puppet with a revolting habit: what was its name?

9 What is the world's most-watched cycling competition?

10 Who wrote the music for the musicals *Cats* and *Starlight Express*?

ANSWERS

1. Serena and Venus 2. Gotham City 3. Yorkshire 4. Clark Kent
5. Scotland 6. Take That 7. John McEnroe 8. Spit 9. Tour de France
10. Andrew Lloyd-Webber

QUIZ 130

1 Which children's programme once featured John Noakes, Lesley Judd and Peter Duncan?

2 How many points would you score if you made a maximum break in snooker?

3 Who played the Penguin in the film *Batman Returns*?

4 Which TV show made Pamela Lee Anderson a star?

5 What square is diagonally opposite the 'Go to Jail' square on a Monopoly board?

6 In which sport would you find a jack and a mat?

7 On which radio station would you find the *Today* programme and *The Archers*?

8 What bird is the symbol of the French rugby team?

9 Which ex-Arsenal and England striker had his own chat show?

10 Of which band is Damon Albarn the lead singer?

ANSWERS

1. *Blue Peter* 2. 147 3. Danny DeVito 4. *Baywatch* 5. Jail 6. Bowls 7. Radio Four 8. A cockerel 9. Ian Wright 10. Blur

QUIZ 131

. . . .

1 What is the name of the bear in *The Muppets*?

2 For which country does Brian Lara play cricket?

3 What cat is always looking to catch and eat Tweetie-Pie?

4 Who plays football at The Dell?

5 In what sort of building is the TV show *ER* set?

6 If you are out for no runs in cricket, what is it called?

7 Which children's programme features Grover and Big Bird?

8 What show about aliens and conspiracies features agent Mulder?

9 What is the name given to the first shot in a tennis rally?

10 Which sport features downhill and slalom competitions?

ANSWERS

1. Fozzie 2. West Indies 3. Sylvester 4. Southampton 5. A hospital 6. A duck
7. *Sesame Street* 8. *The X Files* 9. Serve 10. Skiing

QUIZ 132

1 Which sport features the teams Utah Jazz and Chicago Bulls?

2 Which boy band was named after the London postcode from where they came?

3 What is the name give to someone who runs onto a sports pitch with no clothes on?

4 Which female singer had hits with 'Honey to a Bee' and 'Girlfriend'?

5 In football, what is the small rectangle inside the penalty area called?

6 Which TV soap is set in and around the town of Chester?

7 Who is lead singer of the band REM?

8 Which county cricket side has wicketkeeper Jack Russell played for all his career?

9 What nationality is rugby player Jonah Lomu?

10 Who hosts the TV series *Robot Wars*?

ANSWERS

1. Basketball in America 2. E17 3. A streaker 4. Billie Piper 5. Six yard box
6. *Hollyoaks* 7. Michael Stipe 8. Gloucestershire 9. New Zealand 10. Craig
Charles and Philippa Forrester

QUIZ 133

● ●

1 What was the name of the newspaper Superman worked on?

2 Who plays at the Noucamp stadium?

3 Who directed the first *Batman* film?

4 In which sport does a cox control his or her team?

5 Which sport includes the teams Buffalo Bills, Miami Dolphins and the Washington Redskins?

6 Name Kermit the frog's cousin who sang 'Halfway up the Stairs'?

7 Who was the captain of the French 1998 World Cup football side?

8 Which Hollywood film awards are held before the Oscars?

9 In which city was the first World Club Football Championship held?

10 In which new-romantic band did former *EastEnders* star Martin Kemp once play?

ANSWERS

1. *The Daily Planet* 2. Barcelona football club 3. Tim Burton 4. Rowing
5. American Football 6. Robin 7. Zinedine Zidane 8. The Golden Globes
9. Rio, Brazil 10. Spandau Ballet

QUIZ 134

. . . .

1　Which male German tennis player retired from the game in 1999?

2　Which computer game requires the player to arrange different-shaped falling blocks?

3　Which sport features a quarterback and touchdowns?

4　Which swimming stroke is named after an insect?

5　Which band features brothers Noel and Liam?

6　How many yellow cards equal a red card in football?

7　Which country joined rugby's Five Nations in 2000 to make it Six Nations?

8　With what sport is the venue Twickenham associated?

9　Which duck often accompanies Bugs Bunny in cartoons?

10　Which throwing event involves spinning a ball on a metal chain?

ANSWERS

1. Boris Becker 2. Tetris 3. American Football 4. Butterfly 5. Oasis 6. Two
7. Italy 8. Rugby Union 9. Daffy 10. The hammer

QUIZ 135

1 How many golf shots would you have taken if you had got an eagle?

2 The Superfurry Animals and The Stereophonics hail from which country?

3 Which TV channel broadcasts *Home and Away*, *Rosie and Jim* and *Wheel of Fortune*?

4 How many wickets must you take in cricket to have bowled a side out?

5 What sort of musical instrument are Farfisa and Hammond examples of ?

6 What position in rugby union usually carries the number 15 on the player's shirt?

7 Neil Buchanan hosts which popular TV crafts show for kids?

8 Who became the third most expensive football transfer in Britain when he moved from Leicester to Liverpool?

9 Sam Smith was the number one Briton at which sport?

10 Who did Leeds United beat to progress to the quarter finals of the 2000 UEFA cup?

ANSWERS

1.Three 2.Wales 3.ITV 4.Ten 5.Electric organ 6.Full Back 7.*Art* 8.Emile Heskey 9.Women's Tennis 10.Roma

QUIZ 136

1 Which TV show features characters called Ned Flanders and Mr Burns?

2 Who is the female narrator on the *Teletubbies* show?

3 Which South African cricketer is nicknamed Zulu?

4 What is the name of the BBC radio show based in the fictional town of Ambridge?

5 What did Manchester United replace six times between 1998 and 2000?

6 Which radio station featured live commentary of England's tour of South Africa in 1999/2000?

7 What is the name of the dog in the TV show *Frasier*?

8 What is cricketer Merv the Swerve's real name?

9 What is the name of the character voiced by soul singer Isaac Hayes in *South Park*?

10 Which band had a hit 1999 album with 'The Man Who'?

ANSWERS

1. *The Simpsons* 2. Toyah Wilcox 3. Lance Klusener 4. *The Archers* 5. Their pitch 6. TalkSport Radio 7. Eddie 8. Merv Hughes, Australian fast bowler 9. Chef 10. Travis

QUIZ 137

1 In which position did Australian rugby star David Campese mainly play?

2 Which Beatle provided the narration for *Thomas the Tank Engine*?

3 With which sport was Brazilian Ayrton Senna connected?

4 Which actress plays teenage boy Perry alongside Harry Enfield?

5 Where were the 1980 Summer Olympics held?

6 Which singer hosted the one-off TV show *Victoria's Secrets*?

7 Which villain did Jack Nicholson play in *Batman*?

8 In athletics, what is 4.9 metres long and made of glass fibre?

9 How many points does a team get for an unconverted try in rugby union?

10 Who won an Oscar for his role in the film *Philadelphia*?

ANSWERS

1. Wing 2. Ringo Starr 3. Formula One 4. Kathy Burke 5. Moscow, Russia
6. Victoria Beckham (Posh Spice) 7. The Joker 8. A pole vault pole 9. Five
10. Tom Hanks

QUIZ 138

. . . .

1 Who was the England manager at the 1998 World Cup Finals?

2 Which English player was sent off in the quarter finals of that competition?

3 Which team were England playing at the time?

4 How many people were in the band Steps?

5 Which cartoon character is always chasing Yogi Bear?

6 Which long-running duo's first hit was 'West End Girls'?

7 For which country do footballers Emmanuel Petit and Patrick Vierra play?

8 How many overs do each side get in international one-day cricket matches?

9 Which singer played Tiffany in *EastEnders*?

10 They used to be called football linesmen; what are these officials now called?

ANSWERS

1. Glenn Hoddle 2. David Beckham 3. Argentina 4. Five 5. Ranger Smith
6. Pet Shop Boys 7. France 8. 50 9. Martine McCutcheon 10. Referee's assistants

QUIZ 139

1 Which female singer used to be in a duo with her husband Sonny Bono?

2 How many stations are there on a Monopoly board?

3 Which chess piece is sometimes called a rook?

4 Who has a brother called Niles and a producer of his radio show called Ros?

5 What is the tennis score, technically known as 40-40, called?

6 Who is the star of the computer game *Tomb Raider*?

7 What is the symbol on all Ferrari motor racing cars?

8 Which American comedy drama about a law firm is named after the character played by Calista Flockart?

9 Which former England World Cup star managed the Republic of Ireland for many years?

10 Which children's programme about animals was hosted by Nick Baker and Michaela Strachan?

ANSWERS

1. Cher 2. Four 3. Castle 4. Frasier Crane 5. Deuce 6. Lara Croft
7. A prancing horse 8. *Ally McBeal* 9. Jackie Charlton 10. *The Really Wild Show*

QUIZ 140

1. Which singing group featured Faye, H, Lee, Claire and Lisa?
2. How long is a regular football match?
3. Which character has appeared in *The World is Not Enough* and *Thunderball*?
4. From what country does football star Dennis Bergkamp come?
5. Which band recorded 'Yellow Submarine', 'Help!' and 'A Hard Day's Night'?
6. In snooker, how many points is the green ball worth?
7. Which American comedy show featured Chandler, Monica and Joey?
8. Are boy band Another Level British, Canadian or American?
9. What type of instrument is a Fender Stratocaster?
10. Name one of the two packs of cards in the middle of a Monopoly board.

ANSWERS

1. Steps 2. 90 minutes 3. James Bond 4. The Netherlands 5. The Beatles
6. Three 7. *Friends* 8. British 9. An electric guitar 10. Chance and
Community Chest

QUIZ 141

. . . .

1   Which Scottish comedian starred alongside Judi Dench in *Mrs Brown*?

2   How many shots under par is an eagle in golf?

3   For which NBA basketball team did Michael Jordan play?

4   Which friend of Liz Hurley played the male lead in *Notting Hill*?

5   Where does the Scotland rugby union team play their home games?

6   Who played Judge Dredd in the film of the same name?

7   Which Scottish football team plays at Ibrox?

8   Which American actor starred in *Hook, Dead Poets' Society* and *The Fisher King*?

9   What was the name of the cartoon character known as the friendly ghost?

10 Which band features Thom Yorke as lead singer?

ANSWERS

1. Billy Connolly 2. Two 3. Chicago Bulls 4. Hugh Grant 5. Murrayfield
6. Sylvester Stallone 7. Celtic 8. Robin Williams 9. Casper 10. Radiohead

QUIZ 142

- -

1 Which country was the first to field a father and son in a football world cup game?

2 Which actress played the lead role in the comedy *Gimme, Gimme, Gimme*?

3 Who were England's last opponents in the 1999 cricket world cup?

4 What was the catchphrase of the male lead character in *One Foot in the Grave*?

5 Who is the actor who played him?

6 In which country did Gary Lineker finish his football-playing days?

7 Which Geordie boy band had a hit with the single 'Stand Tough'?

8 Which ex-captain of Scotland plays football for Coventry?

9 Which All Saints' single featured in the film *The Beach*?

10 Who was caretaker manager of the England team between Glenn Hoddle and Kevin Keegan?

ANSWERS

1. Iceland 2. Kathy Burke 3. India 4. 'I don't believe it!' 5. Richard Wilson
6. Japan 7. Point Break 8. Gary McAllister 9. 'Pure Shores'
10. Howard Wilkinson

QUIZ 143

1 What is the maximum number of points allowed in the card game pontoon?

2 Which films feature a cowboy called Woody and Mr Potato Head?

3 Five brothers re-formed their 1970's group in 2000 around their most successful member, Michael. What is that group's name?

4 Which chess piece can only move one space at a time?

5 Which singing star recorded a controversial version of the Lord's Prayer for Christmas 1999?

6 Which band had hits with 'Champagne Supernova' and 'Wonderwall'?

7 How many points is a red ball worth in snooker?

8 From what country does golfer Sergio Garcia come?

9 Who won the 1999 Cricket World Cup?

10 Which film series featured M and Miss Moneypenny?

ANSWERS

1. 21 2. *Toy Story* and *Toy Story 2* 3. The Jackson Five 4. King 5. Cliff Richard
6. Oasis 7. One 8. Spain 9. Australia 10. The Bond films

QUIZ 144

1 Which British Grand Prix driver, the son of a famous racing father, retired in 1999?

2 Which comedian is famous for his impressions of Des Lynam, Dale Winton and Tony Blair?

3 What is the first name of Michael Schumacher's motor-racing younger brother?

4 Who hosts the show *A Question of Sport*?

5 Which sport did she used to play?

6 How many picture cards in a regular pack of cards?

7 Which popular TV comedy series stared Matthew Perry as Chandler Bing?

8 Name the band that features singer Jay Kay?

9 For which country do cricketers Grant Flower and Heath Streak play?

10 In which long-running comedy show did the character of Frasier first appear?

ANSWERS

1. Damon Hill 2. Rory Bremner 3. Ralf 4. Sue Barker 5. Tennis 6. 12
7. *Friends* 8. Jamiroqui 9. Zimbabwe 10. Cheers

QUIZ 145

1 In which town was the TV comedy *Cheers* set?

2 Which new American Football team fought the 2000 Superbowl against the Rams?

3 Who directed the films *Annie Hall*, *Mighty Aphrodite* and *Hannah and her Sisters*?

4 In which city do the Royle family live?

5 What was Muhammad Ali's original name?

6 Which punk rock band were managed by Malcolm McClaren and had a hit with 'Pretty Vacant'?

7 Who is the world champion at chess?

8 What do Monaco, Brands Hatch and Monza have in common?

9 Which modern artist is famous for using sheep, cows and sharks in his art?

10 In pontoon or blackjack, how many points is a king worth?

ANSWERS

1. Boston 2. Tennessee Titans 3. Woody Allen 4. Manchester 5. Cassius Clay
6. Sex Pistols 7. Vladimir Kramnik 8. They are all Grand Prix race tracks
9. Damien Hirst 10. Ten

QUIZ 146

• •

1 Which is the most common piece on a chess board?

2 Name one of the two countries that co-hosted the 2002 Football World Cup.

3 Who was in love with Kermit the Frog in *The Muppets*?

4 What game is played on horseback by, among others, Prince Charles?

5 What football position is associated with Neville Southall, Peter Shilton and Nigel Martyn?

6 Who is Britain's number two tennis player?

7 Which seven-a-side sport features Goal Shooters, Goal Defence and Wing Attack positions?

8 In which city was the TV soap *Brookside* set?

9 Which national cricket side do Wasim Akram and Saqulain Mushtaq play for?

10 In which sport do players use rackets to hit a shuttle?

ANSWERS

1. Pawns 2. Japan and Korea 3. Miss Piggy 4. Polo 5. Goalkeeper 6. Greg Rusedski 7. Netball 8. Liverpool 9. Pakistan 10. Badminton .

QUIZ 147

1 Which Australian spin bowler overtook Dennis Lillee's wicket-taking record in 1999?

2 What type of instrument are crash, ride and high-hat examples of?

3 Which English football team plays at The Valley?

4 Which famous composer wrote 'Twinkle Twinkle Little Star' at the age of four?

5 What is a table tennis ball made of?

6 What type of event would you be watching if you saw an arabesque and a glissade being performed?

7 How many goals did Pelé score in his career: 800, 1200 or 2000?

8 Which sport features a line backer and a wide receiver?

9 What is the surname of the computer game character Crash?

10 Hibs and Hearts are two Scottish football teams: in which city are they based?

ANSWERS

1. Shane Warne 2. Cymbals 3. Charlton Athletic 4. Mozart 5. Celluloid
6. Ballet 7. 1200 8. American Football 9. Bandicoot 10. Edinburgh

QUIZ 148

• •

1 Which director made many suspense films including *Vertigo* and *The Birds*?

2 Which Swedish golfer partnered Sergio Garcia in the 1999 Ryder Cup?

3 Who took over from Sara Cox on Radio One's breakfast show?

4 Which two brothers were in England's 1966 football World Cup-winning team?

5 Which band once featured Phil Collins and Peter Gabriel as lead singers?

6 Which spoof superhero film featured comedian Eddie Izzard as Disco Tony?

7 For which football team did Trevor Sinclair play before his transfer to West Ham?

8 Which actor starred in *The Full Monty*, *Carla's Song* and *Trainspotting*?

9 If you potted all the colour balls in snooker, excluding the reds, how many points would you score?

10 Name the two actors who played the *Men Behaving Badly*.

ANSWERS

1. Alfred Hitchcock 2. Jesper Parnevik 3. Chris Moyles 4. Bobby and Jackie Charlton 5. Genesis 6. Mystery Men 7. Queens Park Rangers 8. Robert Carlyle 9. 27 10. Neil Morrissey and Martin Clunes

QUIZ 149

1. Which Formula One team had the drivers Eddie Irvine and Johnny Herbert in the 2000 season?

2. Which team lost the 1999 cricket world cup final?

3. Who had hits with 'Baby One More Time' and 'Sometimes'?

4. What sort of knights appear in the *Star Wars* films?

5. Who won the 1999 Worthington Cup?

6. With which sport do you associate commentator Murray Walker?

7. What is the name of the eldest kid in *Rugrats*?

8. What is the name of the cat in *Sabrina the Teenage Witch*?

9. What sport uses a foil or an épée?

10. Which boy band released the album 'Invincible'?

ANSWERS

1. Jaguar 2. Pakistan 3. Britney Spears 4. Jedi 5. Tottenham Hotspur
6. Motor racing 7. Angelica 8. Salem 9. Fencing 10. Five

QUIZ 150

1 What type of fruit come in varieties called Cox's Orange Pippin and Granny Smith's?

2 Are whales fish or mammals?

3 How long does an unborn human baby spend inside its mother?

4 Which part of your body features a pupil and a cornea?

5 Which mammal makes large dams out of wood?

6 Is a prickly pear a type of tree, cactus or wallflower?

7 What are the names of the two types of elephant?

8 Which type of bird would you find in a gaggle?

9 What is the name given to a female pig?

10 Which land animal is the fastest runner?

ANSWERS

1. Apples 2. Mammals 3. Nine months 4. The eye 5. The beaver 6. A cactus
7. Indian and African 8. Geese 9. Sow 10. The cheetah

QUIZ 151

• •

1 Which big cat lives the longest: the lion, the panther or the tiger?

2 Can a dog see colours?

3 What is the eye-problem myopia better known as?

4 How many species of acacia tree are there: 15, 60 or 1,200?

5 Which common bird has house, hedge and tree varieties?

6 Gorillas are found in how many continents?

7 The goliath beetle holds which insect record?

8 What adult creature's body contains 206 bones?

9 What is the largest living creature in the world?

10 Which part of a fish is made from spines covered in skin?

ANSWERS

1. The lion 2. No 3. Short-sightedness 4. 1,200 5. Sparrow 6. One
7. The heaviest insect 8. Humans 9. The blue whale 10. Fins

QUIZ 152

• •

1 Hydroponics is the science of growing plants without what usual component?

2 If a creature is extinct, what does it mean?

3 What is the claw of a bird of prey called?

4 What name is often given to a male horse under the age of four?

5 What is the name given to a male giraffe?

6 Which is the longest-living animal?

7 Can it live up to 120, 135 or 180 years?

8 The fossa is a catlike hunter that only lives on which African island?

9 What sort of creature was a New Zealand moa?

10 What is the name given to the female part of a creature, which produces eggs?

ANSWERS

1. Soil 2. It no longer exists 3. Talon 4. Colt 5. Bull 6. The giant tortoise
7. 180 years 8. Madagascar 9. A bird 10. The ovary

QUIZ 153

1 How many arms does an octopus have?

2 What type of creature comes in varieties called hammerhead and great white?

3 How many years can a lion live to: 12, 20 or 30?

4 Are mammals warm- or cold-blooded?

5 Which cuddly Australian creature lives only on eucalyptus leaves?

6 Do conifers produce flowers?

7 Which substance transports oxygen and nutrients around the human body?

8 What is a baby deer called?

9 Do all insects lay eggs?

10 What is the name given to an elephant's long pointed teeth?

ANSWERS

1. Eight 2. The shark 3. 30 4. Warm-blooded 5. The koala 6. No 7. Blood
8. A fawn 9. Yes 10. Tusks

QUIZ 154

• •

1   Are a hundredth, a fiftieth or a quarter of all the world's plants endangered?

2   What name is often given to a female horse under the age of four?

3   Would you find gorillas in their natural habitat, in Africa, Europe, Asia or in all three?

4   What sort of creature is an ocelot?

5   What part of the human body secretes saliva?

6   What common name is often given to the sternum bone in humans?

7   Is a lobelia a plant, an insect or a virus?

8   Which creature carries the disease malaria?

9   What name is given to the art of growing miniature trees and shrubs?

10   What is the outer covering of a tree's trunk called?

ANSWERS

1. A quarter 2. Filly 3. Africa 4. A cat 5. The salivary gland 6. Breast bone
7. A plant 8. Mosquito 9. Bonsai 10. Bark

QUIZ 155

1 The goldcrest bird holds which British record?

2 Does the spruce tree produce hardwood or softwood?

3 Where does a hamster store grain and seeds?

4 What sort of creature is a natterjack?

5 What does an omnivore eat?

6 Are humans omnivores?

7 What is a young kangaroo called?

8 Where does an amphibian live?

9 For what does a rhinoceros use its single horn?

10 Which part of the human body acts as a powerful pump?

ANSWERS

1. It is the smallest British bird 2. Softwood 3. In its cheeks 4. A toad
5. Plants and meat 6. Yes 7. A joey 8. In water and on land 9. Self defence
10. The heart

QUIZ 156

• •

1 Which African creature is related to the horse and has distinctive black-and-white striped markings?

2 Which country is the natural home of the Tasmanian devil?

3 What is the name of the fringe of hair that runs down a horse's neck?

4 What type of animal are Friesian and Jersey?

5 A peregrine falcon can reach 290 km/h in a dive. True or false?

6 Which part of our bodies holds air when we breathe?

7 Which part of a cow stores milk?

8 How many kidneys does the human body normally contain?

9 What name is given to a fox's tail?

10 Arteries carry what from the heart?

ANSWERS

1. Zebra 2. Australia 3. Mane 4. Cows 5. True 6. Lungs 7. The udder 8. Two
9. Brush 10. Blood

QUIZ 157

. . . .

1   Which is the largest member of the cat family?

2   Which white bird is considered the 'bird of peace'?

3   Does the bulb of an onion grow below or above ground?

4   When is a nocturnal animal at its busiest?

5   Which part of a plant takes in water?

6   Which is larger: the alligator or the crocodile?

7   Which is the only poisonous snake found in Britain?

8   How many livers does the human body have?

9   Gorillas stick their tongues out to show anger. True or false?

10 What period of inactivity in winter do many mammals, including hedgehogs, go into?

ANSWERS

1. The tiger 2. Dove 3. Below ground 4. At night 5. Its roots 6. The crocodile 7. The adder (or viper) 8. One 9. True 10. Hibernation

QUIZ 158

- -

1. Which part of a rhubarb plant is poisonous?

2. Through which body part do fish breathe?

3. What does an invertebrate not have?

4. What substance makes leaves green?

5. Which mammal has the heaviest brain: a sperm whale, a human or an elephant?

6. Do entomologists study skin, insects or flowering plants?

7. What is a baby elephant called?

8. In which continent would you find alligators in their natural habitats?

9. How does a python kill its prey?

10. Do cucumbers grow below or above ground?

ANSWERS

1. Its leaves 2. Gills 3. A backbone 4. Chlorophyll 5. A sperm whale
6. Insects 7. Calf 8. North America 9. By crushing 10. Above ground

QUIZ 159

- -

1　Penguins are only found in one continent: which is it?

2　Where is a rattlesnake's rattle?

3　In which continent would you find giant pandas and the snow leopard?

4　Which type of animal are spaniels and beagles?

5　What are the two types of squirrel that live in Britain?

6　Can an emu fly?

7　Where do veins carry blood back to?

8　In which continent would you find llamas?

9　Do olives grow under the ground, on trees or on small flowering plants?

10　Which tree provides conkers in autumn?

ANSWERS

1. Antarctica 2. In its tail 3. Asia 4. Dogs 5. Red and grey squirrel 6. No
7. The heart 8. South America 9. On trees 10. Horse chestnut

QUIZ 160

• •

1 Which is the world's largest bird?

2 How tall can an adult giraffe stand: 2.5 metres, 3.5 metres or 5.5 metres?

3 What type of creature comes in varieties including fruit and vampire?

4 What is the scientific name for the large intestine?

5 Which is the largest penguin: the blue, the Adélie or the Emperor?

6 Is a chimpanzee a primate?

7 How many humps does a dromedary camel have?

8 Can a sea cucumber move?

9 Is the tail fin of a fish called the caudal fin, the dorsal fin or the pelvic fin?

10 Are knee joints hinge, ball and socket or sliding joints?

ANSWERS

1. The ostrich 2. 5.5 metres 3. Bat 4. Colon 5. Emperor penguin 6. Yes
7. One 8. Yes, it can slide along the sea floor 9. Caudal fin 10. Hinge joints

QUIZ 161

• •

1   Which ape is covered in reddish fur and has very long limbs to swing through trees?

2   What pet is a domesticated form of the South American cavy?

3   Where in your body would you find metacarpal bones?

4   What does the pitcher plant eat?

5   In which part of your body would you find the cochlea and three semi-circular canals?

6   How many legs does a lobster have?

7   What is the human body's largest organ?

8   Which creature has the largest eye in the animal kingdom?

9   Is that eye 13, 37 or 52 centimetres in diameter?

10 Is the tamarisk a tree, an insect or a small monkey?

ANSWERS

1. Orang-utan 2. Guinea pig 3. Hands 4. Insects 5. The ear 6. Ten 7. The skin 8. Giant squid 9. 37 centimetres 10. A tree

QUIZ 162

. . . .

1   How many legs does a tapir have?

2   What is the only native British tree with a name starting with O?

3   What is a young pig called?

4   How long can a cockroach live without a head: one minute, one hour, one day or one week?

5   Which type of dog is associated with the Queen?

6   The cabbage family of plants includes broccoli and radishes. True or false?

7   What is the full name for a budgie?

8   How many arms does a starfish normally have?

9   What is a male cow called?

10 How many bones are there in a human neck: 7, 17 or 70?

ANSWERS

1. Four 2. Oak 3. Piglet 4. One week 5. Corgi 6. True 7. Budgerigar 8. Five
9. Bull 10. 7

QUIZ 163

1 In which part of the body is waste stored before being pushed out of the anus?

2 Which bird has the biggest wingspan?

3 Is the mouse deer of Asia a real deer or not?

4 How tall does it grow: 25 centimetres, 1 metre or 1.5 metres high?

5 Which peacock has an incredible set of tail feathers: the male or the female?

6 How much food can an adult hippo eat overnight: 1, 10 or 100 kilograms?

7 Is bamboo a tree or a grass?

8 Is an echidna a lizard, a small mammal or a type of beetle?

9 What measurement is used for the height of horses?

10 Which vegetable did Mark Twain describe as a 'cabbage with a college education'?

ANSWERS

1. Rectum 2. The albatross 3. It is a real deer 4. 25 centimetres high 5. The male peacock 6. 100 kilograms 7. A grass 8. A small mammal 9. Hands 10. Cauliflower

QUIZ 164

. . . .

1　How many humps does a Bactrian camel have?

2　What are camels' humps used for?

3　Is the male part of a flower called a stigma, ovule or stamen?

4　How many kilograms of plants can an adult elephant eat in a day?

5　How is an ocelot's coat patterned?

6　What type of sea creature is a Portuguese man-of-war?

7　What can a chameleon do with its eyes which most animals cannot?

8　Which part of their bodies do hippos use to pluck grass out of the ground?

9　Are avocados fruits or vegetables?

10　Which two countries boast different species of echidna?

ANSWERS

1. Two 2. As a fat store 3. Stamen 4. 110 kilograms 5. With spots
6. A jellyfish 7. Move them in different directions at the same time
8. Their lips 9. Fruit 10. Australia and New Zealand

QUIZ 165

• •

1 Tawny and barn are types of which bird?

2 How many leaves does a lucky clover have?

3 Do wild gerbils live in deserts, forests or on the African plains?

4 Do hippos eat fish?

5 Does a giraffe have more, fewer or the same number of neck bones as a human?

6 What is a female lion called?

7 Which bird lays the largest eggs?

8 What is a young bear called?

9 What colour do stoats turn in winter?

10 What is an anaconda?

ANSWERS

1. Owl 2. Four 3. Deserts 4. No 5. The same number 6. Lioness 7. Ostrich
8. A cub 9. White 10. A snake

QUIZ 166

. . . .

1 Which is the slowest: a domestic cat, an elephant or a squirrel?

2 What other name is often give to the aubergine?

3 Do leopards mainly hunt at night or during the day?

4 Which is the fastest: a black mamba snake, a chicken or a pig?

5 How much water can a male giraffe drink in a day: 14 litres, 20 litres or 48 litres?

6 As a fraction, how much of the human body is made up of water?

7 Is a persimmon a fruit, an insect, a vegetable or a lizard?

8 Through which season do estivating animals sleep?

9 What are roe?

10 What is a Venus flytrap?

ANSWERS

1. A squirrel 2. Eggplant 3. At night 4. A black mamba snake 5. 48 litres
6. $^2/_3$ 7. A fruit 8. Summer 9. The eggs of fish 10. A fly-eating plant

QUIZ 167

1 Which is the fastest: a grizzly bear, a human or a giraffe?

2 How long, in months, is the pregnancy of a white rhino?

3 What is the proper term for a young wolf?

4 Which food is botanically a fruit although it is commercially termed a vegetable?

5 Which monkey is a favoured prey of the leopard?

6 Apart from humans, name one of the two natural enemies of hippos?

7 What is the name used for a male swan?

8 Approximately how many giant pandas exist: 1,000, 10,000 or 100,000?

9 Three quarters of the dust in a typical home consists of what?

10 Which is the longest bone in the human body?

ANSWERS

1. A giraffe 2. 18 3. Pup 4. Tomato 5. Baboon 6. Lions and crocodiles
7. Cob 8. 1,000 9. Dead skin cells 10. The thigh bone or femur

QUIZ 168

. . . .

1   What are Basmati and Patna forms of?

2   Is a jaguar a member of the cat or dog family?

3   In which continent would you find jaguars?

4   Which other Australian animal is the wallaby closely related to?

5   From which animal do we get ham and bacon?

6   Which typical cat feature is missing from the Manx cat?

7   Which is the world's biggest shark: the whale shark, the great white shark or the tiger shark?

8   What kinds of creature are red admiral and cabbage white?

9   What is the nest where bees make honey called?

10 Which fruit is commonly used to make wine?

ANSWERS

1. Rice 2. Cat family 3. North America 4. Kangaroo 5. Pig 6. A tail
7. The whale shark 8. Butterflies 9. A hive 10. Grapes

QUIZ 169

1 What is another name for the trachea?

2 Does the male or female mosquito actually bite people?

3 What do bees collect from flowers to help make honey?

4 Is a peccary a wild pig, an insect collection or a small flowering bush?

5 Which type of creature do ospreys eat?

6 How many milk teeth does a human have as a child?

7 How many adult teeth are the milk teeth replaced by?

8 Are there over 1,000, over 600 or over 250 muscles in the human body?

9 How are the seeds of a dandelion dispersed?

10 Are spiders or fruit flies part of the arachnid family?

ANSWERS

1. The windpipe 2. Female mosquito 3. Nectar 4. A wild pig 5. Fish 6. 20
7. 32 8. Over 600 9. By wind 10. Spiders

QUIZ 170

1 What name is given to a plant that completes its life cycle in one year?

2 Which word describes a female swan?

3 How tall can a giant sunflower grow: one, three or eight metres?

4 What is the largest artery travelling from the human heart called?

5 Which salad vegetable was for many years considered poisonous?

6 The world consumption of which household product uses 29,160 hectares of woodland every day?

7 Dendochronology is the study of which part of a tree?

8 For how long does a honey bee live: six weeks, six months or six years?

9 The milk of which female farm animal is used to make feta cheese?

10 The sapodilla tree's sap is used to make which popular product?

ANSWERS

1. Annual 2. Pen 3. Three metres 4. Aorta 5. Tomato 6. Toilet paper
7. The rings in a tree's trunk 8. Six weeks 9. Sheep 10. Chewing gum

QUIZ 171

. . . .

1 How many wings does a bee have: two, four or six?

2 Which mammal feeds entirely on ants?

3 Do insects have more or fewer legs than spiders?

4 If someone was examining your cranium, what part of your body would they be looking at?

5 Which creature boasts the biggest ears in the world?

6 Is a cygnet a young goose, duck or swan?

7 Is the chihuahua the smallest breed of dog?

8 Which is the only mammal that can fly?

9 Haricot, mung and butter are all types of what?

10 What are the fruits of an oak tree called?

ANSWERS

1. Four 2. Anteater 3. Fewer 4. Head 5. African elephant 6. Swan 7. Yes 8. The bat 9. Bean 10. Acorns

QUIZ 172

● ●

True or false:

1 The tarantula is the most poisonous spider.

2 Rhinos are placid creatures with poor eyesight.

3 Bald-headed eagles have bald heads.

4 Dolphins sleep at night just below the surface of the water.

5 Lions will attack hippos.

6 Capsicum is another word for black peppercorns.

7 No two zebras have the same pattern of stripes.

8 Warthogs can run at speeds of 50 km/h.

9 Owls can turn their heads through 360 degrees.

10 Ostriches bury their heads in the sand when scared.

ANSWERS

1. False 2. True 3. False 4. True 5. True 6. False 7. True 8. True 9. False
10. False

QUIZ 173

. . . .

True or false:

1 The duck-billed platypus is the only mammal to lay eggs.

2 Leopards will attack elephants.

3 When a baby kangaroo is born it is no bigger than a human thumb.

4 Lynx is another name for mountain lion.

5 Male mouth-brooding frogs carry the eggs of their young in vocal sacs.

6 The potato is closely related to the tomato and the bell pepper.

7 Ostriches are capable of digesting rocks and dirt.

8 A group of kangaroos is called a mob.

9 Veal comes from sheep.

10 A jellyfish is 95 percent water.

ANSWERS

1. False 2. False 3. True 4. False 5. True 6. True 7. True 8. True 9. False 10. True

QUIZ 174

• •

True or false:

1 Brussels sprouts are miniature cabbages.

2 15,000 species of living thing are becoming extinct every year.

3 The cheetah can run at speeds of over 100 km/h.

4 Ostriches are today bred for their meat.

5 A domesticated otter is called a polecat.

6 Lettuce was considered a weed by the Romans.

7 The water vole is the smallest mammal in Britain.

8 Carrots belong to the parsley family.

9 The meat of a rabbit is called venison.

10 Basil is a herb related to mint.

ANSWERS

1. False 2. True 3. True 4. True 5. False 6. True 7. False 8. True 9. False
10. True

QUIZ 175

. . . .

1   Do echidnas lay eggs?

2   How many legs does a crab have?

3   How many million times does your heart beat in a year?

4   Which part of a chameleon is as long as its body?

5   Dogs can make around 10 distinctive sounds. How many more can a cat make?

6   On what kind of tree do catkins grow?

7   Is an anteater an African or South American animal?

8   Which colour is the flower of the common poppy?

9   Is a leech a type of worm, scorpion or fly?

10 In which organ in the human body would you find the stirrup and anvil bones?

ANSWERS

1. Yes 2. Ten 3. 37 million 4. Its tongue 5. More than 90 more 6. Hazel
7. South American 8. Red 9. Worm 10. The ear

QUIZ 176

· ·

1 What is the largest living thing on Earth?

2 How many litres of blood does an adult human body contain?

3 Which domesticated animal is descended from *Felis silvestris*?

4 What is *Rafflesia arnoldi* the largest example of in the world?

5 In which Asian country would you find it?

6 In which river would you find the biggest crocodiles of all?

7 How many metres long can they grow to?

8 Dian Fossey is associated with the study and conservation of which animal?

9 Do hippos have tusks?

10 The narwhal has a spike protruding from its head. What is it made of?

ANSWERS

1. A tree (the sequoia) 2. Five 3. The cat 4. Flower 5. Indonesia 6. The Nile
7. Six 8. Gorillas 9. Yes 10. Ivory

QUIZ 180

. . . .

[tru]ffles are a form of fungi. Name a well-known
[ed]ible fungi beginning with M.

[W]hat is a male duck called?

[W]hich creature creates natural silk?

[Is] a roach a freshwater or saltwater fish?

[W]hat word describes a female tiger?

[W]hich vegetable can make us cry when we peel
[a]nd cut it?

[W]hich type of animal has species called grey,
[h]umpback and sperm?

[H]ow many different species of elephant are
there?

What are the two main ingredients of
mayonnaise?

Which creature can contain a natural pearl inside
its shell?

ANSWERS

[1].Mushroom 2.Drake 3.Silkworm 4.Freshwater 5.Tigress 6.Onion
[7].Whale 8.Two 9.Eggs (egg yolks) and oil 10.An oyster

QUIZ 177

. . . .

1 How many toes does a hippo have on each hoof?

2 What is a female fox called?

3 What animal are Siamese and Burmese breeds of?

4 The meat of which animal provides T-bone and
   sirloin steaks?

5 Soya is used as a meat substitute. What sort of
   plant is soya?

6 The giant kelp is the longest example of which
   marine plant?

7 What name is given to a male chicken?

8 Name any one of three native British trees
   beginning with the letter A.

9 Which tree has bright red berries and spiked
   leaves and is associated with Christmas?

10 Is a perch a freshwater or saltwater fish?

ANSWERS

1.Four 2.Vixen 3.Cat 4.Cow 5.A bean 6.Seaweed 7.Rooster 8.Ash,
alder or aspen 9.Holly 10.Freshwater

QUIZ 178

1 Hippos have been responsible for killing more than 400 people in Africa. True or false?

2 How much of the day do koalas sleep: 2 hours, 4 hours, 12 hours or 18 hours?

3 Which is the only big cat that lives in social groups?

4 How many stomachs does a camel have?

5 The duck-billed platypus is the only mammal that is poisonous. True or false?

6 For what are your incisor teeth used?

7 What colour is the blood of squid and octopuses?

8 The jellylike substance in some bones has the same name as a type of large vegetable; what is it?

9 What name is given to trees that bear cones?

10 Which bird builds an eyrie as a nest?

ANSWERS

1. True 2. 18 hours 3. The lion 4. Four 5. True 6. Cutting food 7. Blue
8. Marrow 9. Conifers 10. Eagle

QUIZ 1

1 Do the petals of the world's larg measure 20 cm, 30 cm or 50 cm

2 What is the world's largest land

3 To the nearest 50 kg, how much male of this species weigh?

4 Can a narwhal's spike grow to one metres in length?

5 What are your molar teeth used for

6 Which sea creature with a sting has brain?

7 How do squid move through the wa propulsion, by swimming with their te by drifting with the water flow?

8 What do most white blood cells do in body?

9 Is balsa classified as a softwood or hardw

10 Which part of the sorrel plant do human

ANSWERS

1. 50 centimetres 2. The polar bear 3. 650 kilograms 4. Three metres
5. Grinding food up 6. Jellyfish 7. Jet propulsion 8. Fight germs
9. Hardwood 10. The leaves

QUIZ 181

• •

1 The Scots pine is the most commonly used tree in Britain for which purpose?

2 A jack ass is a male ass; what is a female called?

3 Is a banyan a type of antelope, a tree or a small insect?

4 Do truffles grow above or below ground?

5 The deadly funnel-web spider is found in which country?

6 What word is used to describe a male rabbit?

7 What is unusual about the seeds of a strawberry?

8 Are frogs and newts amphibians?

9 Which organ filters blood, removing water and other molecules in the human body?

10 The Arctic tern holds which bird record?

ANSWERS

1. As a Christmas tree 2. Jenny 3. A tree 4. Below ground 5. Australia
6. Buck 7. They grow on the outside of the fruit 8. Yes 9. Kidneys
10. Longest bird migration

QUIZ 182

• •

1 What is the largest creature in the world without a backbone?

2 Seventy percent of all animals have three body parts and three sets of legs. What are these animals?

3 Of which type of teeth does an adult human have a maximum of four?

4 Which word describes the technique of preventing human fertilization?

5 Queen termites hold which insect record?

6 Which part of many plants is concerned with reproduction?

7 What is the middle part of an insect's body called?

8 The spine-tailed swift is the world's fastest bird in level flight. How fast can it travel?

9 How many months does an elephant spend inside the mother before being born: 8–10, 14–16, 20–22 or 30–32?

10 Is the average life span of an ostrich longer than a lion?

ANSWERS

1. Giant squid 2. Insects 3. Canines or wisdom 4. Contraception 5. Longest living 6. The flower 7. Thorax 8. 170 km/h 9. 20–22 months 10. Yes

QUIZ 183

1. Colorado and death watch are types of which creature?

2. What is the name of a rabbit's burrow?

3. Is a mandrill a parrot, a monkey or an insect?

4. What happens to a deciduous tree in autumn?

5. Does the polar bear live in the Arctic or Antarctic?

6. Do sloths defecate once a day, once every three days or once a week?

7. What name is given to a female dog?

8. Is a halibut a saltwater or freshwater fish?

9. Two thirds of a shark's brain is devoted to which sense?

10. Where would you find your Achilles tendon?

ANSWERS

1. Beetle 2. A warren 3. A monkey 4. Its leaves fall off 5. The Arctic 6. Once a week 7. Bitch 8. Saltwater 9. Smell 10. On the heel of your foot

QUIZ 184

1 Which part of your tongue can taste sweet things?

2 What is a baby goose called?

3 Which British bird is an electric blue colour and is famous for its sudden dives into rivers?

4 Does the insect called a midge beats its wings 62, 620 or 62,000 times a minute?

5 What is the main food of the giant panda?

6 What kind of animal is a Gloucester Old Spot?

7 Do sharks ever eat their own young?

8 Wombats are only found on which island off Australia?

9 Can dingoes bark?

10 Does the boxwood tree produce hardwood or softwood?

ANSWERS

1. The front tip 2. Gosling 3. Kingfisher 4. 62,000 5. Bamboo shoots
6. A pig 7. Yes, sometimes 8. Tasmania 9. No 10. Hardwood

QUIZ 177

1 How many toes does a hippo have on each hoof?

2 What is a female fox called?

3 What animal are Siamese and Burmese breeds of?

4 The meat of which animal provides T-bone and sirloin steaks?

5 Soya is used as a meat substitute. What sort of plant is soya?

6 The giant kelp is the longest example of which marine plant?

7 What name is given to a male chicken?

8 Name any one of three native British trees beginning with the letter A.

9 Which tree has bright red berries and spiked leaves and is associated with Christmas?

10 Is a perch a freshwater or saltwater fish?

ANSWERS

1. Four 2. Vixen 3. Cat 4. Cow 5. A bean 6. Seaweed 7. Rooster 8. Ash, alder or aspen 9. Holly 10. Freshwater

QUIZ 178

1 Hippos have been responsible for killing more than 400 people in Africa. True or false?

2 How much of the day do koalas sleep: 2 hours, 4 hours, 12 hours or 18 hours?

3 Which is the only big cat that lives in social groups?

4 How many stomachs does a camel have?

5 The duck-billed platypus is the only mammal that is poisonous. True or false?

6 For what are your incisor teeth used?

7 What colour is the blood of squid and octopuses?

8 The jellylike substance in some bones has the same name as a type of large vegetable; what is it?

9 What name is given to trees that bear cones?

10 Which bird builds an eyrie as a nest?

ANSWERS

1. True 2. 18 hours 3. The lion 4. Four 5. True 6. Cutting food 7. Blue
8. Marrow 9. Conifers 10. Eagle

QUIZ 179

1 Do the petals of the world's largest flower measure 20 cm, 30 cm or 50 cm across?

2 What is the world's largest land predator?

3 To the nearest 50 kg, how much can an adult male of this species weigh?

4 Can a narwhal's spike grow to one, two or three metres in length?

5 What are your molar teeth used for?

6 Which sea creature with a sting has no heart or brain?

7 How do squid move through the water: by jet propulsion, by swimming with their tentacles or by drifting with the water flow?

8 What do most white blood cells do in the human body?

9 Is balsa classified as a softwood or hardwood?

10 Which part of the sorrel plant do humans eat?

ANSWERS

1. 50 centimetres 2. The polar bear 3. 650 kilograms 4. Three metres
5. Grinding food up 6. Jellyfish 7. Jet propulsion 8. Fight germs
9. Hardwood 10. The leaves

QUIZ 180

1 Truffles are a form of fungi. Name a well-known edible fungi beginning with M.

2 What is a male duck called?

3 Which creature creates natural silk?

4 Is a roach a freshwater or saltwater fish?

5 What word describes a female tiger?

6 Which vegetable can make us cry when we peel and cut it?

7 Which type of animal has species called grey, humpback and sperm?

8 How many different species of elephant are there?

9 What are the two main ingredients of mayonnaise?

10 Which creature can contain a natural pearl inside its shell?

ANSWERS

1. Mushroom 2. Drake 3. Silkworm 4. Freshwater 5. Tigress 6. Onion
7. Whale 8. Two 9. Eggs (egg yolks) and oil 10. An oyster

QUIZ 184

1 Which part of your tongue can taste sweet things?

2 What is a baby goose called?

3 Which British bird is an electric blue colour and is famous for its sudden dives into rivers?

4 Does the insect called a midge beats its wings 62, 620 or 62,000 times a minute?

5 What is the main food of the giant panda?

6 What kind of animal is a Gloucester Old Spot?

7 Do sharks ever eat their own young?

8 Wombats are only found on which island off Australia?

9 Can dingoes bark?

10 Does the boxwood tree produce hardwood or softwood?

ANSWERS

1. The front tip 2. Gosling 3. Kingfisher 4. 62,000 5. Bamboo shoots
6. A pig 7. Yes, sometimes 8. Tasmania 9. No 10. Hardwood

QUIZ 183

．．．．．．．．．．．．．．．．．．．．．．．．．．

1 Colorado and death watch are types of which creature?

2 What is the name of a rabbit's burrow?

3 Is a mandrill a parrot, a monkey or an insect?

4 What happens to a deciduous tree in autumn?

5 Does the polar bear live in the Arctic or Antarctic?

6 Do sloths defecate once a day, once every three days or once a week?

7 What name is given to a female dog?

8 Is a halibut a saltwater or freshwater fish?

9 Two thirds of a shark's brain is devoted to which sense?

10 Where would you find your Achilles tendon?

ANSWERS

1. Beetle 2. A warren 3. A monkey 4. Its leaves fall off 5. The Arctic 6. Once a week 7. Bitch 8. Saltwater 9. Smell 10. On the heel of your foot

QUIZ 185

1. An elephant's trunk contains 40,000 muscles. True or false?

2. Which North American animal is the largest member of the deer family?

3. Which B word means relating to the cow or buffalo?

4. What is a male bee without a sting called?

5. Belladonna is another name for which poisonous British plant?

6. Which two animals are crossed to form a mule?

7. How many claws facing forward and how many backward does a parrot have?

8. Where would you find heartwood in a tree?

9. Does the pygmy shark, growing just 20 centimetres long, exist?

10. How far can grey kangaroos jump in a single bound: 6, 9, 14 or 30 metres?

ANSWERS

1. True 2. Moose 3. Bovine 4. A drone 5. Deadly nightshade 6. A horse and a donkey 7. Two forward and two backward 8. In the centre of the tree's trunk 9. Yes 10. 14 metres

QUIZ 186

1 Mayflies live for just two hours. True or false?

2 Are birds warm or cold-blooded?

3 Topiary is the art of clipping what into fancy shapes?

4 Do slugs have one, four or fifty noses?

5 What sort of creature is an anaconda?

6 On what part of your body are your taste buds?

7 Can a hummingbird fly backwards as well as forwards?

8 Does food travel through your stomach or large intestine first?

9 Where would you find a clavicle bone: your shoulder, your foot or your wrist?

10 Are tulips grown from seeds or bulbs?

ANSWERS

1. True 2. Warm-blooded 3. Hedges and trees 4. Four 5. A snake 6. Your tongue 7. Yes 8. Stomach 9. Your shoulder 10. Bulbs

QUIZ 187

- -

1 What is the first name of Tony Blair's wife?

2 Which silent film actor played the part of the little tramp?

3 In which country was Adolf Hitler born?

4 Was Marilyn Monroe a singer, actress or painter?

5 In which military force did Douglas Bader fight?

6 In the Bible, who led the animals in 'two by two'?

7 Harry Webb is the real name of which long-running pop singer?

8 Which wartime prime minister had the nickname Winnie?

9 What was the first name of Hardy, of Laurel and Hardy fame?

10 What nationality was Leonardo da Vinci?

ANSWERS

1. Cherie 2. Charlie Chaplin 3. Austria 4. Actress 5. The RAF 6. Noah 7. Cliff Richard 8. Winston Churchill 9. Oliver 10. Italian

QUIZ 188

• •

1 Which British boxer fought Mike Tyson in Manchester in January 2000?

2 Is Al Murray a comedian, a singer or a professional golfer?

3 In which profession has David Lean achieved fame?

4 Which painter's most famous work is *The Haywain*?

5 Which singer-songwriter once used to be in the pop duo Wham!?

6 What outstanding facial feature did Cyrano de Bergerac have?

7 Which American comedian played an updated version of Cyrano in the film *Roxanne*?

8 For what did Philip Larkin become famous?

9 Which famous Tudor explorer wrote a history of the world while imprisoned in the Tower of London?

10 Which female criminal was found guilty of the Moors Murders?

ANSWERS

1. Julius Francis 2. A comedian 3. Film directing 4. John Constable
5. George Michael 6. A huge nose 7. Steve Martin 8. Poetry 9. Sir Walter
Raleigh 10. Myra Hindley

QUIZ 189

• •

1 Which American president was romantically linked with Marilyn Monroe?

2 What were the surnames of the two English writers of comic operettas?

3 In Roman mythology, who was the messenger of the gods?

4 Which former *Carry On* star has played the landlady of *EastEnders'* pub, The Queen Vic?

5 Who was the first person to fly solo across the Atlantic?

6 What was the name of his aircraft?

7 Who made over 1,000 inventions, including the phonograph and practical electric lighting?

8 Which country did he come from?

9 What is the real name of punk singer Johnny Rotten?

10 Which political party did Sir James Goldsmith form in 1994?

ANSWERS

1. John F Kennedy 2. Gilbert and Sullivan 3. Mercury 4. Barbara Windsor
5. Charles Lindbergh 6. *Spirit of St Louis* 7. Thomas Edison 8. The United
States 9. John Lydon 10. The Referendum Party

QUIZ 190

• •

1 Who owns the Virgin business empire?

2 In which sort of craft has he tried to circumnavigate the globe?

3 What was the first name of Laurel, of Laurel and Hardy fame?

4 From which country does the comedian Billy Connolly come?

5 What did Glenda Jackson do before she became an MP?

6 Which political party does she represent?

7 Who painted the *Mona Lisa*?

8 Who is the patron saint of England?

9 Which figure in the Bible fought Goliath?

10 With what device did he fight?

ANSWERS

1. Richard Branson 2. Balloon 3. Stan 4. Scotland 5. She was an actress
6. Labour Party 7. Leonardo da Vinci 8. St George 9. David 10. A slingshot

QUIZ 191

. . . .

1 Which actor and heart-throb played the male lead in *Titanic*?

2 Who was the actress and singer daughter of Judy Garland?

3 To which actor and director was Emma Thompson once married?

4 Who was Ronald Reagan's vice president?

5 Reg Dwight is the real name of which singer?

6 Which politician earned the nickname The Iron Lady?

7 Cherilyn Sarkisian shortened her name and became a famous singer: who is she?

8 What was the name of her husband and co-singer?

9 Fred Lasby was the oldest person to do what in an aircraft?

10 What nationality was Pablo Picasso?

ANSWERS

1. Leonardo Di Caprio 2. Liza Minnelli 3. Kenneth Branagh 4. George Bush
5. Elton John 6. Margaret Thatcher 7. Cher 8. Sonny Bono 9. Fly round the world 10. Spanish

QUIZ 192

• •

1 What does the 'F' in John F Kennedy's name stand for?

2 Who was the first bowler to take 300 test wickets?

3 What type of drink does Oz Clark write about?

4 Who is the current editor of *Private Eye*?

5 On which long-running news quiz show does he appear?

6 What did King Alfred the Great allegedly burn?

7 Which king was murdered in Pontefract Castle?

8 Who is the patron saint of France: St Pierre, St Denis or St Michel?

9 Gertrude Ederle was the first woman to do what in 1926?

10 William Booth founded which 'army'?

ANSWERS

1. Fitzgerald 2. Fred Trueman 3. Wine 4. Ian Hislop 5. *Have I Got News For You?* 6. The cakes 7. Richard II 8. St Denis 9. Swim the English Channel 10. The Salvation Army

QUIZ 193

. . . .

1 Who hosted *Supermarket Sweep* and other game shows?

2 Which tennis player has been romantically linked to Barbra Streisand?

3 To which action hero was actress Demi Moore married?

4 What does Michael Fish do on television?

5 Which king was known as The Lionheart?

6 Who married Prince Edward in 1999?

7 Which composer wrote *The Four Seasons*?

8 For which sport did Michael Jordan become famous?

9 What was the surname of the singers Donny, Marie, Jay and Jimmy?

10 How many people attended Mozart's funeral: 1, 40, 100 or 1,000?

ANSWERS

1. Dale Winton 2. Andre Agassi 3. Bruce Willis 4. He is a weatherman
5. Richard I 6. Sophie Rhys-Jones 7. Vivaldi 8. Basketball 9. Osmond
10. 1

QUIZ 194

• •

1   Who is the patron saint of Wales?

2   Which film saw the first acting performance of footballer Vinnie Jones?

3   To which British tennis player was Chris Evert once married?

4   With what sort of vehicle was Barry Sheene associated?

5   Who was Prince Charles' best man at his wedding to Diana?

6   OJ Simpson once played which sport professionally?

7   Which series of spoof detective films did he star in alongside Leslie Nielsen?

8   Which heavyweight boxer was once married to Robin Givens?

9   Which popular sport was devised by James Naismith?

10 Who succeeded Edward VII after he abdicated?

ANSWERS

1. St David 2. *Lock, Stock and Two Smoking Barrels* 3. John Lloyd
4. Motorcycles 5. He didn't have one 6. American Football 7. *The Naked Gun* 8. Mike Tyson 9. Basketball 10. George VI

QUIZ 195

. . . .

1 Which film star's real name was Norma Jean Baker?

2 Which jazz singer and trumpeter was nicknamed Satchmo?

3 Which country did Ian Smith lead?

4 What has Ang Rita Sherpa done more times than any other person?

5 Which British prime minister said 'You've never had it so good'?

6 The Rosetta Stone gave the key to Egyptian hieroglyphics. Where is it now?

7 Which fashion designer has made clothes for Madonna and used to star on *Eurotrash*?

8 Which famous Hollywood star gave her name to a type of lifejacket?

9 What did the Russian dictator Stalin study at university?

10 Which Anita founded the Body Shop company?

ANSWERS

1. Marilyn Monroe 2. Louis Armstrong 3. Rhodesia 4. Climbed Everest without oxygen 5. Harold Macmillan 6. In the British Museum 7. Jean-Paul Gaultier 8. Mae West 9. Theology 10. Anita Roddick

QUIZ 196

1 Who wrote *The Planets* suite?

2 What nationality was he: German, Czech or British?

3 Was the Yorkshire Ripper a real person or a fictional character?

4 Of which company is Bill Gates the president?

5 Which gangster was nicknamed Scarface?

6 What did William Wilberforce fight to abolish?

7 Who was alleged to have said 'We are not amused'?

8 With which instrument is Eric Clapton associated?

9 What was the painter Van Gogh's first name?

10 Which movie actor has the nickname Sly?

ANSWERS

1. Gustav Holst 2. British 3. A real person 4. Microsoft 5. Al Capone
6. Slavery 7. Queen Victoria 8. Electric guitar 9. Vincent
10. Sylvester Stallone

QUIZ 197

1. Which European country had a leader by the name of King Zog?

2. Which famous movie star had the nickname Duke?

3. What bit Queen Elizabeth II in 1991?

4. With what campaign is the name Emily Pankhurst associated?

5. Which Southampton football player was appointed manager of Wales?

6. Which Hollywood film star became mayor of the town of Carmel?

7. How much was he paid per year for the job: $200, $2,000, $20,000 or $200,000?

8. Which singing star's real name is Annie Mae Bullock?

9. Who was woken in bed in 1982 by intruder Michael Fagan?

10. What did John Loudon McAdam improve?

ANSWERS

1. Albania 2. John Wayne 3. One of her corgi dogs 4. Votes for women
5. Mark Hughes 6. Clint Eastwood 7. $200 8. Tina Turner 9. Queen
Elizabeth II 10. Roads

QUIZ 198

1 Was Frank Sinatra once married to Mia Farrow, Lulu or Cher?

2 Who was the inventor of the *Peanuts* cartoon strip?

3 Which international statesman received the Nobel Peace Prize in 1990?

4 What did Mary Read do for a living?

5 What was the profession of American Frank Lloyd Wright?

6 Of which country was Archbishop Makarios the first president?

7 What nationality was Prince Henry the Navigator?

8 Which threatened author made a surprise appearance at a 1993 U2 concert?

9 What weapon was Sir Barnes Wallis famous for building?

10 In which year did Prince Charles and Lady Diana Spencer marry?

ANSWERS

1. Mia Farrow 2. Charles Schulz 3. Mikhail Gorbachev 4. She was a pirate
5. Architect 6. Cyprus 7. Portuguese 8. Salman Rushdie 9. A bouncing
bomb 10. 1981

QUIZ 199

1 What is Sporty Spice, Mel C,'s real name?

2 Which Australian soap started the careers of Jason Donovan and Kylie Minogue?

3 Who was the man behind the cartoon characters Mickey Mouse and Donald Duck?

4 Which John has been Minister for Transport and is nicknamed Two Jags?

5 What nationality was the painter Claude Monet?

6 Was he: a cubist, an impressionist or a Renaissance artist?

7 Which famous singer-songwriter was born Robert Zimmerman?

8 In which year was Prince William born: 1973, 1976, 1982 or 1986?

9 Is he older or younger than his brother Harry?

10 The artist Frans Hals painted a famous picture of a cavalier – what was the cavalier doing?

ANSWERS

1. Melanie Chisholm 2. *Neighbours* 3. Walt Disney 4. John Prescott 5. French
6. Impressionist 7. Bob Dylan 8. 1982 9. Older 10. Laughing

QUIZ 200

1 Which fascist leader of Italy was nicknamed *Il Duce*?

2 Which sports presenter transferred from BBC to ITV in 1999?

3 What kind of tax was William Pitt famous for introducing in 1799?

4 What were the Romans Virgil, Ovid and Horace famous for?

5 'Thank God I have done my duty' were the last words of which naval war hero?

6 Which British 400-metre runner was a BMX bike champion as a child?

7 Which millionaire ran for American president as an independent in 1992?

8 What was the name of the Yorkshire Ripper?

9 Who is estimated to be the richest person in the world?

10 Which pop group of brothers, who had hits with 'ABC' and 'One Bad Apple', included Michael and Jermaine?

ANSWERS

1. Mussolini 2. Des Lynam 3. Income tax 4. Writing poetry 5. Lord Nelson
6. Iwan Thomas 7. Ross Perot 8. Peter Sutcliffe 9. Bill Gates 10. The Jacksons or Jackson Five

QUIZ 201

1 Which film director was Mia Farrow married to up until the 1990s?

2 In which Oscar-winning film did she appear, married to Michael Caine?

3 How much did Bill Gates buy the computer operating system Ms-DOS for: $75,000, $7.5 million or $75 million?

4 For which artform is Barbara Hepworth known?

5 Who shot and killed Lee Harvey Oswald?

6 The Neville brothers are famous footballers. What does their sister, Tracy, play for England?

7 What is the first name of the Nevilles' father?

8 Which Scottish actor received a knighthood in the 1999 New Year's Honours list?

9 Of which political party was Jeremy Thorpe once a leader?

10 Peach Melba got its name from which opera singer?

ANSWERS

1. Woody Allen 2. *Hannah and her Sisters* 3. $75,000 4. Sculpture 5. Jack Ruby 6. Netball 7. Neville 8. Sean Connery 9. The Liberal Party 10. Dame Nellie Melba

QUIZ 202

• •

1   Which philosopher wrote *Das Kapital*, which inspired many generations of communists?

2   What are both the Gibbs and Leslie pairs of brothers famous for playing?

3   Which artist of the 1960s and 1970s shortened his name from Andrew Warhola?

4   After which saint is Santa Claus named?

5   Which ancient king had a round table?

6   Which religious leader lives in the Vatican City?

7   How many brothers does Princess Anne have?

8   Were the Two Fat Ladies cooks, book critics or travel show presenters?

9   Which Judy played Dorothy in the film version of *The Wizard of Oz*?

10 Was André Previn a comedian, painter, violinist or conductor?

ANSWERS

1. Karl Marx 2. Rugby union 3. Andy Warhol 4. St Nicholas 5. King Arthur
6. The pope 7. Three 8. Cooks 9. Judy Garland 10. A conductor

QUIZ 203

• •

1 Mohamed Al-Fayed owns which famous store?

2 Which jazz musician was known as Bird?

3 Did he play the jazz guitar, the saxophone or the trumpet?

4 Who was the first wife of William Shakespeare?

5 How many middle names does Prince William have?

6 Which communist philosopher's dying words were 'Last words are for fools who haven't said enough'?

7 Which minister was involved in the 'Profumo Affair'?

8 In which era did a figure called Jack the Ripper terrorize London?

9 About whom was the musical *Evita* written?

10 In which country did she live?

ANSWERS

1. Harrods 2. Charlie Parker 3. The saxophone 4. Anne Hathaway 5. Three
6. Karl Marx 7. John Profumo 8. The Victorian era 9. Eva Perón
10. Argentina

QUIZ 204

• •

1 Which king of England couldn't speak any English?

2 Which writer won the Pulitzer prize in 1952 for his book *The Old Man and the Sea*?

3 What was Margaret Bondfield the first woman to do in 1929?

4 Who was the only bachelor president of the United States?

5 Which former Tory party member is a famous author and once ran for Mayor of London?

6 Which countess is considered the world's first computer programmer?

7 Was the computer language FORTH, ADA or COBOL named in her honour?

8 Which two comedians starred on the *Fantasy Football League* TV show?

9 Which English middle-distance runner became a Conservative MP in the 1990s?

10 Which star of the films *Mona Lisa* and *Hannah and Her Sisters* was originally called Maurice Micklewhite?

ANSWERS

1. George I 2. James Buchanan 3. Become the first female cabinet minister
4. James Buchanan 5. Jeffrey Archer 6. Countess Ada Lovelace 7. ADA
8. David Baddiel and Frank Skinner 9. Sebastian Coe 10. Michael Caine

QUIZ 205

1 Which brothers flew their aeroplane from Kitty Hawk in 1903?

2 Which tough-guy actor had the nickname Bogey?

3 Which famous pop drummer's real name is Richard Starkey?

4 With which classical musical instrument is Nigel Kennedy associated?

5 Jim Henson provided the puppets for which famous children's show?

6 In 2004, who wore the number 23 shirt for Real Madrid Football Club?

7 What standard facial feature is missing from the *Mona Lisa* painting?

8 What is Sean Connery's real first name: Titus, Thomas or Timothy?

9 Which group of brothers would you be watching if you could see Harpo, Zeppo and Groucho?

10 Was Carlos the Jackal a film character, a terrorist or an enemy of the Crusades?

ANSWERS

1. The Wright Brothers 2. Humphrey Bogart 3. Ringo Starr 4. The violin
5. *The Muppets* 6. David Beckham 7. Eyebrows 8. Thomas 9. The Marx Brothers 10. A terrorist

QUIZ 206

• •

1 Who invented the Baygen radio, which requires no batteries?

2 Which winner of the 1996 Rugby World Cup received the trophy from Nelson Mandela?

3 In which band was Michael Hutchence the lead singer and songwriter?

4 Who was the girlfriend of Michael Hutchence at the time of his death?

5 Which Boomtown Rat had she been married to previously?

6 Name the actress and MP who was an early candidate in the election for the mayor of London?

7 What have union leader Jimmy Hoffa, aviator Amelia Earhart and Lord Lucan all got in common?

8 To which actress was Humphrey Bogart married?

9 Which computing device did Douglas J Englebart invent: the hard disk, the joystick, the mouse or the microprocessor?

10 Which two politicians contested the nomination as Labour Party candidate for the mayor of London?

ANSWERS

1. Trevor Baylis 2. François Pienaar 3. INXS 4. Paula Yates 5. Bob Geldof
6. Glenda Jackson 7. They all disappeared and have never been traced
8. Lauren Bacall 9. The mouse 10. Frank Dobson and Ken Livingstone

QUIZ 207

. . . .

1 Who wrote the novel *The Great Gatsby*?

2 Who was the first person to meet Christ after the crucifixion?

3 Which pianist and composer wrote 'Maple Leaf Rag' and other ragtime songs?

4 Whose famous art studio in the 1960s was called The Factory?

5 Which cartoonist's first job was drawing pictures for a barber, receiving 25 US cents or a free haircut per picture?

6 Which Peter's biography, full of stories of his acting and writing days, was called *Just Me*?

7 Dashiell Hammett created which tough, fictional detective?

8 If your surname is Cooper, historically what would you have been?

9 If you were nicknamed Dusty, what would your surname most likely be?

10 Which American male tennis player was known as Superbrat?

ANSWERS

1. F Scott Fitzgerald 2. Mary Magdalene 3. Scott Joplin 4. Andy Warhol
5. Walt Disney 6. Peter Ustinov 7. Sam Spade 8. A barrel maker 9. Miller
10. John McEnroe

QUIZ 208

1 What is the nationality of snooker player Stephen Hendry?

2 How did flying ace Douglas Bader lose his legs?

3 What sport did he become very good at in later life?

4 With which sport would you associate father and son, Harry and Jamie Redknapp?

5 Soul singer Natalie Cole had an even more famous singing father: who was he?

6 Which captain did Princess Anne marry in the 1970s?

7 What nationality is Jesse Jackson?

8 Has he ever run for president of the United States?

9 How much did the heaviest man in Britain, Peter Yarnall, weigh when he died: 278, 328 or 368 kilograms?

10 What did Sir Edmund Hillary conquer?

ANSWERS

1. Scottish 2. In a flying accident 3. Golf 4. Football 5. Nat King Cole
6. Mark Phillips 7. American 8. Yes 9. 368 kilograms 10. Mount Everest

QUIZ 209

1 Noir is the French word for which colour?

2 Who is the patron saint of Scotland?

3 What is the home of a wolf called?

4 Who was the wife of Kurt Cobain at the time of his death?

5 Which wheelchair-bound physicist, famous for his work on black holes, has motor neurone disease?

6 Which car maker once said 'History is bunk'?

7 Was OJ Simpson found guilty or innocent of killing his wife?

8 Which German engineer, called Willy, gave his surname to a range of World War II aircraft?

9 Who owns *The Sun* and *The Times* newspapers?

10 Which Russian communist leader's name had the meaning 'man of steel'?

ANSWERS

1. Black 2. St Andrew 3. Lair 4. Courtney Love 5. Stephen Hawking
6. Henry Ford 7. Innocent 8. Messerschmitt 9. Rupert Murdoch 10. Stalin

QUIZ 210

· ·

1 For what did Howling Wolf and Big Mama Thornton become famous?

2 Was Cameron MacIntosh is a famous Australian politician, Scottish politician, theatre impresario or film director?

3 Which film ogre married Princess Fiona?

4 Who was the British doctor found guilty of killing his patients?

5 Who is the patron saint of Ireland?

6 To which American political party does Newt Gingrich belong?

7 Who plays Sir Les Patterson and Dame Edna Everage?

8 Which Australian supermodel has the nickname The Body?

9 Who was Elvis Presley's manager?

10 Who, in a four-year period, made 300 inventions, one every five days?

ANSWERS

1. Singing the blues 2. Theatre impresario 3. Shrek 4. Dr Harold Shipman
5. St Patrick 6. Republican 7. Barry Humphries 8. Elle Macpherson
9. Colonel Tom Parker 10. Thomas Edison

QUIZ 211

1. In the Bible, what were the names of Adam's two sons?

2. Was Sir Christopher Wren an architect, a prime minister or a naval captain?

3. Who is the patron saint of travellers, an image of whom is often worn around the neck?

4. Is Henry Moore known as a sculptor, a poet, a playwright or a painter?

5. Which US president was known as Honest Abe?

6. Whom did Melinda, a product manager at Microsoft, marry in 1994?

7. Who is the heir to the British throne?

8. Which one of the following is not a current Labour MP: Neil Kinnock, Robin Cook, Tony Blair, Jack Straw?

9. Who sentenced Jesus to death?

10. How was writer, Herbert George Wells, better known?

ANSWERS

1. Cain and Abel 2. An architect 3. St Christopher 4. A sculptor 5. Abraham Lincoln 6. Bill Gates 7. Prince Charles 8. Neil Kinnock 9. Pontius Pilate 10. HG Wells

QUIZ 212

1 Which film actress was married to Tom Cruise?

2 Which saint is commemorated on February 14th?

3 Carl Sagan was noted for his work in which scientific field?

4 Which US state is home to the Disney theme parks in Orlando?

5 How many garages does Bill Gates' house have: 3, 5, 9 or 35?

6 During the Gulf War, what was the nickname of military man, HN Schwarzkopf?

7 Painter Paul Gauguin lived and painted on which South Pacific island?

8 Which one of the following was not a member of the Monty Python team: Terry Jones, Terry Gilliam, Marty Feldman, Graham Chapman?

9 Who is current holder of the title Princess Royal?

10 How old was Minie Monroe when she married a man of 83 in 1991?

ANSWERS

1. Nicole Kidman 2. St Valentine 3. Planetary science 4. Florida 5. 35
6. Stormin' Norman 7. Tahiti 8. Marty Feldman 9. Princess Anne 10. 103

QUIZ 213

1 Is Tracy Emin a soul singer, a choreographer or a modern artist?

2 To which actress is director Blake Edwards married?

3 Which Australian media owner organized a rebel cricket competition?

4 Which Victorian engineer had the initials IKB?

5 Which former Yorkshire batsman now gives expert cricket analysis on Talk Radio?

6 Matthew and John are two of the Gospels; can you name the other two?

7 Runner Derek Redmond is married to which famous swimmer?

8 What was the surname of the twins who terrorised the east end in the 1960s?

9 And which pair of brothers portrayed them on film?

10 Which ex-Beatle is a member of the Travelling Wilburys band?

ANSWERS

1. A modern artist 2. Julie Andrews 3. Kerry Packer 4. Isambard Kingdom Brunel 5. Geoffrey Boycott 6. Luke and Mark 7. Sharron Davies 8. The Krays 9. The Kemps, Martin and Gary 10. George Harrison

QUIZ 214

1 Who did England beat in the final of the 2003 Rugby Union World Cup?

2 If you were with Naomi, Claudia and Elle, would you most likely be at a fashion show, on a theatre stage or playing at a pop concert?

3 What was Mussolini's first name?

4 What is the name of Prince Andrew's eldest daughter: Zara, Eugenie or Beatrice?

5 Did Henry Matisse became famous as a classical composer, an opera singer or a painter?

6 Who was Frank James' more famous outlaw brother?

7 On which sport did Harry Carpenter commentate for more than fifty years?

8 Which limb did Lord Nelson lose in battle?

9 John McCarthy and Terry Waite were held captive in which Middle Eastern country?

10 What was the first name of Nelson Mandela's first wife?

ANSWERS

1. Australia 2. A fashion show 3. Benito 4. Beatrice 5. A painter 6. Jesse James 7. Boxing 8. His right arm 9. Lebanon 10. Winnie

QUIZ 215

. . . .

1 Which motorcycle daredevil's real name was Robert Craig?

2 Who is the patron of the Worldwide Fund for Nature?

3 Who is third in line to the British throne?

4 Which general ruled Spain until his death in 1975?

5 Which US president was nicknamed Ike?

6 Whose wealth is estimated at more than 48 billion dollars?

7 Which famous film actress' brother is Warren Beatty?

8 Name either of the actress daughters of Sir Michael Redgrave?

9 Which Middle Eastern king married and divorced Toni Gardiner?

10 Who was Angelica Huston's famous film director father?

ANSWERS

1. Evel Knievel 2. Prince Philip 3. Prince Harry 4. General Franco
5. Dwight Eisenhower 6. Bill Gates 7. Shirley Maclean 8. Vanessa and Lynn
9. King Hussein of Jordan 10. John Huston

QUIZ 216

1 By what name is Gordon Sumner better known?

2 Who was the Greek slave who wrote a collection of fables?

3 Who is the patron saint of doctors?

4 How old was Daisy Ashford when she wrote *The Young Visiters*: 9, 14, 19 or 90?

5 Which name, beginning with S, was given to the work of artists such as Salvador Dali and René Magritte?

6 Sir Stamford Raffles founded a trading post in which Southeast Asian country?

7 Which Australian feminist wrote *The Female Eunuch*?

8 Which actress, with the original name Joyce Frankenberg, changed her name to the same as one of Henry VIII's wives?

9 What did Lord Nelson lose the use of at the Siege of Calvi in 1794?

10 Who is seventh in line to the British throne?

ANSWERS

1. Sting 2. Aesop 3. St Luke 4. Nine 5. Surrealism 6. Singapore 7. Germaine Greer 8. Jane Seymour 9. His right eye 10. Prince Edward

QUIZ 217

1 Which band was nicknamed The Fab Four?

2 Did Gene Hackman, Gene Kelly or Gene Wilder play Popeye Doyle in the *French Connection* films?

3 With which entertainment has Prince Edward been associated?

4 How many children does Princess Anne have?

5 Which former prime minister has two children called Carol and Mark?

6 What is the first name of Bill and Hillary Clinton's daughter?

7 Which English general gave his name to a type of rubber boot?

8 Actor Tony Booth is the father of which politician's wife?

9 Which wife of King Henry VIII is said to have had six fingers on one hand?

10 Tom Selleck turned down which role in the adventure series of films starting with a lost ark?

ANSWERS

1. The Beatles 2. Gene Hackman 3. Theatre 4. Two 5. Margaret Thatcher
6. Chelsea 7. Duke of Wellington 8. Tony Blair 9. Anne Boleyn 10. Indiana Jones

QUIZ 218

. . . .

1 Who is WAPL Windsor better known as?

2 Which ex-Labour leader has a wife called Glennis?

3 What is the surname of the brothers, one a natural history film-maker, the other an actor and director of films such as *Gandhi*?

4 In 1991, what notable British first did Helen Sharman achieve?

5 For which crime was gangster Al Capone eventually imprisoned?

6 Which British queen was nicknamed Good Queen Bess?

7 Which Conservative Party politician was released from jail in January 2000, wearing an electronic tag?

8 What fear or phobia did both Marilyn Monroe and Howard Hughes have?

9 What did Sir Rowland Hill pioneer in Victorian times?

10 Which fighter pilot's life was portrayed in the film *Reach for the Sky*?

ANSWERS

1. Prince William 2. Neil Kinnock 3. David and Richard Attenborough 4. She was the first British woman in space 5. Income tax evasion 6. Elizabeth I 7. Jonathan Aitken 8. Agoraphobia – fear of open spaces 9. The penny post using postage stamps 10. Douglas Bader

QUIZ 219

. . . .

1 Which religious leader's real name is Karol Jozef Wojtyla?

2 Which film, with the lead played by John Hurt, was about the life of John Merrick?

3 Which member of *Beyond the Fringe* is a medical doctor: Peter Cook, Alan Bennett or Jonathan Miller?

4 Who was the first woman to fly solo from England to Australia?

5 What did John Paul Getty III lose when kidnapped in 1974?

6 Which horse-racing commentator retired in 1997 after 50 years service?

7 Which actress has won a record four Oscars in major roles?

8 Which English king was known as The Unready?

9 In which European country do people not have surnames?

10 Is the word 'beautiful' a verb, an adjective or a noun?

ANSWERS

1. Pope John Paul II 2. *The Elephant Man* 3. Jonathan Miller 4. Amy Johnson
5. His right ear 6. Peter O'Sullivan 7. Katharine Hepburn 8. Ethelred
9. Iceland 10. An adjective

QUIZ 220

1 Was the composer Frederic Chopin English, French, Italian or Polish?

2 Which Paulo pushed a football referee over: Di Canio, Maldini or Wanchope?

3 Thor Heyerdahl sailed on a raft from Polynesia to which country: Peru, Australia or the United States?

4 By which nickname was Emma Bunton better known during the 1990s?

5 Who wrote the music for *The Lion King*: George Michael, Steps, Andrew Lloyd-Webber or Elton John?

6 Which British chat show host is a fully trained and practising lawyer?

7 Jacques Cousteau is associated with which sort of exploration: undersea, mountain, space or jungle?

8 Stanley Gibbons was a dealer in which collectable items?

9 Which pop star did Mark Chapman shoot dead in 1980?

10 Which artist was married to that pop star?

ANSWERS

1. Polish 2. Paulo Di Canio 3. Peru 4. Baby Spice 5. Elton John 6. Clive Anderson 7. Undersea 8. Stamps 9. John Lennon 10. Yoko Ono

QUIZ 221

. . . .

1 Which singer and drummer played the Artful Dodger as a child actor?

2 What do actress Susan Hampshire, writer Hans Christian Andersen and General Patton all have in common?

3 Which US president bought Louisiana from France?

4 By which nickname was Wild West outlaw William Bonney better known?

5 Lady Emma Hamilton caused a stir by having a romantic attachment to which war hero?

6 What was Sir Henry Cole the first to do at Christmas in 1843?

7 Which first name, which rhymes with his surname, did David Bowie give to his son?

8 Which former England football manager co-wrote the *Hazel* detective series?

9 Who was the BBC Sports Personality of the Year, 2001?

10 In which soap is the local newspaper called The Walford Gazette?

ANSWERS

1. Phil Collins 2. They are or were dyslexic 3. Thomas Jefferson 4. Billy the Kid 5. Nelson 6. Send Christmas cards 7. Zowie 8. Terry Venables 9. David Beckham 10. *EastEnders*

QUIZ 222

. . . .

1. Which former news reporter contested and won a seat in Parliament standing as an independent?

2. Which Conservative politician did he defeat at the election?

3. Which jazz singer was known as Lady Day?

4. Who pioneered effective treatments against anthrax and rabies?

5. Malcolm Little changed his surname to include just one letter; what was it?

6. Who was the youngest-ever British prime minister?

7. Who made his money in sugar and financed a famous art gallery in London?

8. Who were Pavlova, Nijinsky and Fonteyn?

9. Which inventor created the three-wheeled electric car after a series of ZX home computers?

10. Who directed the films *ET*, *The Color Purple* and *Jaws*?

ANSWERS

1. Martin Bell 2. Neil Hamilton 3. Billie Holliday 4. Louis Pasteur 5. Malcolm X 6. William Pitt the Younger 7. Sir Henry Tate 8. Ballet dancers 9. Sir Clive Sinclair 10. Steven Spielberg

QUIZ 223

1. Arthur Scargill was a union leader in which industry: coal mining, shipping or teaching?

2. Was Oswald Mosley leader of the British Union of Fascists or the British Communist Party in the 1930s?

3. Was William the Conqueror a Roman, a Saxon or a Norman?

4. Which football team has Michael Owen played for all of his career, so far?

5. Are Lee Hurst and Jack Dee tap dancers, comedians or newsreaders?

6. Which popular duo presented the 2003 Pop Idol TV contest?

7. Is Karl Marx buried in Britain, France or Germany?

8. Was Ian Dury a sculptor, a pop musician or a theatre director?

9. What nationality is the actor Jude Law?

10. How many Oscars has Michael Caine won: none, one or two?

ANSWERS

1. Coal mining 2. British Union of Fascists 3. A Norman 4. Liverpool
5. Comedians 6. Ant and Dec 7. Britain 8. Pop musician 9. British 10. Two

QUIZ 224

1 What weapon were Big Willie and Little Willie the first examples of?

2 What was the colour of the first postage stamp?

3 Which British king was famous for having six wives?

4 Who was the British prime minister before Tony Blair?

5 What does the 'VE' in VE Day stand for?

6 Was Trafalgar a sea, land or air battle?

7 Who commanded the British forces at Trafalgar?

8 In which year did World War I end?

9 In which city did Princess Diana die after a car crash?

10 With which decade was the fashion designer Mary Quant associated?

ANSWERS

1. Tanks 2. Black (the penny black) 3. Henry VIII 4. John Major 5. Victory in Europe 6. A sea battle 7. Lord Nelson 8. 1918 9. Paris 10. The 1960s

QUIZ 225

. . . .

1 Which Roman emperor fiddled while Rome burned?

2 Which creature became extinct in 1680?

3 Which wife of King Henry VIII survived him?

4 In which year did the first person travel into space?

5 In which year did the Suez Canal open?

6 Which emperor did Brutus and Cassius kill in the Roman senate?

7 Who was the first person to reach the South Pole?

8 In which year did President Nixon resign?

9 Which country handed over Florida to the USA in 1819?

10 What were the nationality of kamikaze pilots in World War II?

ANSWERS

1. Nero 2. The dodo 3. Catherine Parr 4. 1961 5. 1869 6. Julius Caesar
7. Roald Amundsen 8. 1974 9. Spain 10. Japanese

QUIZ 226

• •

1 Which nation provided reinforcements to the British at the Battle of Waterloo?

2 Who was the first wife of King Henry VIII?

3 In which English county is the site of the Battle of Edgehill?

4 What type of weapon was a Brown Bess?

5 Which country was historically known as New France?

6 Which space shuttle exploded in flight, killing all crew members?

7 How many children were born to Queen Victoria?

8 Who was Labour Party leader before Tony Blair?

9 In which two countries did the ancient Mayan culture exist?

10 Which royal house did both Edward I and Richard II belong to?

ANSWERS

1. Prussia 2. Catherine of Aragon 3. Warwickshire 4. A type of musket or gun 5. Canada 6. Challenger 7. Seven 8. John Smith 9. Mexico and Guatemala 10. House of Plantagenet

QUIZ 227

1. How many Catherines did King Henry VIII have as wives?

2. What killed King Harold of England?

3. What was unusual about the childhood of Romulus and Remus, the twins who founded Rome?

4. Which American president resigned over a scandal known as Watergate?

5. What type of event was Woodstock?

6. In which decade did it occur?

7. Which king was alleged to have commanded the sea to retreat?

8. Was the Battle of Agincourt a land or sea battle?

9. Who was Queen Victoria's husband?

10. Which frontier wall was built in AD122?

ANSWERS

1. Three 2. An arrow 3. They were brought up by wolves 4. Richard Nixon
5. A music festival 6. The 1960s 7 King Canute 8. A land battle 9. Prince Albert 10. Hadrian's Wall

QUIZ 228

• •

1 Which event started with the assassination of Archduke Franz Ferdinand?

2 Which throne was he heir to?

3 What didn't the British government fund until 1833?

4 In which century was the first photograph taken?

5 What did Eire do in 1949?

6 In which year did James I become king: 1405, 1601 or 1720?

7 By what name is East Pakistan now known?

8 Which empire did Genghis Khan found?

9 What decade saw the arrival of teddy boys and rock 'n' roll?

10 Who was president of France until 1969?

ANSWERS

1. World War I 2. The Austrian 3. Schools 4. The 19th century 5. Declare itself a republic 6. 1601 7. Bangladesh 8. The Mongol Empire 9. The 1950s 10. Charles de Gaulle

QUIZ 229

1 Which important document was signed at Runnymede in the 1200s?

2 Which Indian tribe did Geronimo lead?

3 Who was assassinated in 1968 by James Earl Ray?

4 In which century did Marco Polo visit China?

5 What was the system of picture writing used in ancient Egypt called?

6 What did the Hudson Bay Company, set up in 1680, trade in?

7 Who was the first prime minister of an independent India?

8 Of which country were the Sui, the Han and the Three Kingdoms ruling dynasties?

9 Who was the first Communist leader of the Soviet Union?

10 In which civil war were the battles of Bull Run and Gettysberg?

ANSWERS

1. Magna Carta 2. The Apache 3. Martin Luther King 4. 13th century
5. Hieroglyphics 6. Furs 7. Nehru 8. China 9. Lenin
10. The American Civil War

QUIZ 230

· ·

1   Whose ships were known as longships?

2   Was the Battle of Britain fought on land, sea or in the air?

3   Which ex-prime minister of Britain has a wife called Norma?

4   Around the banks of which river did the ancient Egyptian culture develop?

5   With what sort of vehicle is the term 'stealth' associated?

6   How many women prime ministers has Britain had?

7   How many female presidents of the United States have there been?

8   In which year did World War II start?

9   Was a trireme a Roman warship, a Greek council of war or a Saxon drink?

10 Who lives in a monastery?

ANSWERS

1. Vikings 2. In the air 3. John Major 4. The Nile 5. Military aircraft 6. One
7. None 8. 1939 9. A Roman warship 10. Monks

QUIZ 231

• •

1 Which outlaw was shot by his own gang in 1852?

2 Who was the first president of the United States?

3 What do the initials NATO stand for?

4 What did Britain, Eire and Denmark do in 1973?

5 Which city in Peru was the centre of the Inca empire?

6 What was destroyed by a volcanic eruption in AD79?

7 With which culture do you associate Socrates and Theseus?

8 What happened approximately 24,000 years ago?

9 Which Lady ruled Britain for just nine days?

10 In which year was Nelson Mandela released from prison?

ANSWERS

1. Jesse James 2. George Washington 3. North Atlantic Treaty Organization
4. Joined the European Economic Community 5. Cuzco 6. The city of
Pompeii 7. Ancient Greek 8. The Ice Age 9. Lady Jane Grey 10. 1990

QUIZ 232

• •

1   Who came to the throne when Queen Victoria died?

2   Who did Charlemagne become king of in AD771: the Franks, Goths or Vandals?

3   On which island did Eric the Red establish the first Viking colony?

4   Did he do this in 775, 982 or 1048?

5   Who was nicknamed The Lady of the Lamp?

6   In which war did she tend injured troops?

7   Which famous building in India was completed in 1643?

8   In which year did Prince Charles and Princess Diana agree a divorce?

9   In which year was Pope John Paul II elected?

10 How many popes were there that year?

ANSWERS

1. Edward VII 2. The Franks 3. Greenland 4. 982 5. Florence Nightingale
6. The Crimean War 7. Taj Mahal 8. 1996 9. 1978 10. Three

QUIZ 233

1 What do the initials RAF stand for?

2 In which year was Magna Carta signed: 1180, 1300, 1215 or 1403?

3 Name one of the three countries that boycotted the 1980 Moscow Olympics?

4 Who was United States president before Bill Clinton?

5 What were the Zero, the Me109 and the Spitfire?

6 Which disaster hit London in 1666?

7 What was mead: a type of bread, an alcoholic drink, a simple hut?

8 Who was the younger daughter of Henry VIII?

9 In which decade was the first *Star Wars* film released?

10 Which famous London church was founded by Edward in 1052?

ANSWERS

1. Royal Air Force 2. 1215 3. Kenya, the United States and West Germany
4. George Bush 5. World War II fighter aircraft 6. The Great Fire
7. An alcoholic drink 8. Elizabeth I 9. The 1970s 10. Westminster Abbey

QUIZ 234

1 Which country was Menachem Begin leader of in the 1970s?

2 Who travelled to central Africa to find Dr Livingstone?

3 Which book was completed in 1086?

4 Which island in the South Pacific features 600 mysterious stone head statues?

5 In the War of American Independence, which country joined in on America's side in 1779?

6 Who was Henry VIII's only son?

7 Who was the son's mother?

8 Which Celtic queen led a revolt against the Romans?

9 What was made up of cohorts and legions?

10 With which decade are mini skirts and Carnaby Street associated?

ANSWERS

1. Israel 2. Henry Stanley 3. The Domesday book 4. Easter Island 5. Spain
6. Edward VI 7. Jane Seymour 8. Boudicca 9. Roman armies 10. The 1960s

QUIZ 235

1 Who was the only American president to serve three consecutive terms in office?

2 Which Russian and British leaders was he joined by at the post-World War II Yalta conference?

3 Who was the first king or queen of the House of Windsor?

4 Robert Mugabe became leader of which African country in 1980?

5 Which famous newspaper was published for the first time in 1785?

6 Which party was formed by Anton Drexler in 1919?

7 What happened to Rome in AD455?

8 Which French monarch was known as the Sun King?

9 What depicted the Battle of Hastings in 72 scenes?

10 Who was defeated at Orleans in 1429 by an English army?

ANSWERS

1. Franklin Delano Roosevelt 2. Stalin and Churchill 3. George V
4. Zimbabwe 5. *The Times* 6. The Nazi Party 7. It was destroyed 8. Louis XIV
9. The Bayeaux Tapestry 10. Joan of Arc

QUIZ 236

True or false:

1 The Incas mummified their dead, just like the ancient Egyptians.

2 British television's Channel Four started broadcasting in 1991.

3 The Renaissance was a period of renewed interest in arts and learning starting in the 1300s.

4 1066–1400 is known as the Dark Ages.

5 People first farmed around 10,000 years ago.

6 The Stone Age came before the Bronze Age.

7 Queen Elizabeth's Silver Jubilee was celebrated in 1979.

8 The V2 was a type of German submarine.

9 The first European ship to bring back slaves from West Africa was in 1441.

10 The Great Pyramid of ancient Egypt was the tallest building in the world until the Eiffel Tower was built.

ANSWERS

1. True 2. False 3. True 4. False 5. True 6. True 7. False 8. False 9. True
10. True

QUIZ 237

. . . .

1   Which world leader dramatically resigned on New Year's Eve, 1999?

2   How many American colonies declared their independence in 1776: four, seven or thirteen?

3   Which English city was known to the Vikings as Jorvik?

4   What was the name of Nelson's flagship?

5   In both World War I and World War II, what was an 'ace'?

6   Where did Roman senators meet to discuss matters of state?

7   In which century was the civil war in Britain?

8   Which financial event signalled the start of the Great Depression?

9   How many crusades were there?

10   Which two countries fought the Hundred Years' War?

ANSWERS

1. Boris Yeltsin 2. 13 3. York 4. HMS *Victory* 5. A fighter pilot who had shot down many enemy aircraft 6. The Senate 7. The 17th century 8. The Wall Street Crash 9. Eight 10. England and France

QUIZ 238

. . . .

1 In which World War I battle, lasting 141 days, did the British and French lose 600,000 men?

2 In which year was the last Viking attack on Britain: 980, 1066 or 1100?

3 What was abolished in the British Empire in 1833?

4 From which ship was the first SOS message broadcast?

5 In which year did Adolf Hitler become chancellor of Germany?

6 Which Italian family ruled Florence from the 1400s to the 1700s?

7 In which German town were Nazi war leaders put on trial?

8 In which year was the Hubble Space Telescope launched?

9 What was the name of the Turkish empire which ruled from the 1200s until 1918?

10 What was the Praetorian Guard designed to protect?

ANSWERS

1. The Somme 2. 1066 3. Slavery 4. The *Titanic* 5. 1933 6. The Medici family
7. Nuremberg 8. 1990 9. Ottoman Empire 10. Rome and its emperor

QUIZ 239

. . . .

1   What type of shop first opened in Britain in 1948?

2   Which country was once ruled by shoguns?

3   In which decade did the Gulf War occur?

4   In 1980 which former actor became president of the United States?

5   How many atom bombs have been dropped?

6   Which country did the Germans first invade, starting World War II?

7   What was the nickname given to Baron von Richthofen in World War I?

8   Who crossed the Alps with elephants to attack Rome?

9   What sort of weapons are Scuds and Exocets?

10   Who explored parts of the Americas in 1492?

ANSWERS

1. A supermarket 2. Japan 3. The 1990s 4. Ronald Reagan 5. Two 6. Poland
7. The Red Baron 8. Hannibal 9. Missiles 10. Christopher Columbus

QUIZ 240

1 Which country did Iraq invade to trigger the first Gulf War?

2 Who was the leader of Iraq at the time?

3 Which famous castle held Allied prisoners in World War II?

4 Which Scottish king defeated the English at Bannockburn?

5 Western Europe had NATO, what was Eastern Europe's military alliance called?

6 What is the name for the Roman pictures made out of large numbers of small painted tiles?

7 William I started the construction of which London building in 1078?

8 What was the family name of Henry VII?

9 What was the nickname of King Ivan of Russia?

10 What was discovered in California in 1848, starting a 'rush'?

ANSWERS

1. Kuwait 2. Saddam Hussein 3. Colditz 4. Robert the Bruce 5. Warsaw Pact
6. Mosaics 7. Tower of London 8. Tudor 9. Ivan the Terrible 10. Gold

QUIZ 241

. . . .

1 In which World War II battle did over 100,000 German troops surrender to the Russians?

2 Who was executed in front of Whitehall Palace in 1649?

3 Which tax on part of a house was abolished in Britain in 1851?

4 In which year were the last hangings in Britain?

5 What name was given to the medieval contest featuring two knights on horseback each with a lance?

6 Which 'Great' leader created a vast empire from Greece to India in the period 336–323BC?

7 Which famous English ancient monument was sold at auction in 1915 for £6,600?

8 Which Indian prime minister was assassinated by her own bodyguards in 1986?

9 How large was the army that defeated the Saxons at the Battle of Hastings: 1,200, 5,000, 9,000 or 22,000?

10 Which European country was unified in 1861?

ANSWERS

1. Stalingrad 2. King Charles I 3. Tax on windows 4. 1964 5. Jousting
6. Alexander the Great 7. Stonehenge 8. Indira Gandhi 9. 9,000 10. Italy

QUIZ 242

1 Who was prime minister directly before John Major?

2 Where did Christopher Columbus land in 1498?

3 Who flies in *Air Force One*?

4 What were Sherman and Panzer examples of in World War II?

5 In which century did the French Revolution occur?

6 What in Roman times had a hot room, a warm room and a cold room?

7 In which civil war were the battles of Marston Moor and Naseby?

8 Which new British political party formed in 1981?

9 Which American president was shot dead in a theatre in 1865?

10 Which country did Britain fight over rights to the Falkland Islands?

ANSWERS

1. Margaret Thatcher 2. Mainland America 3. The United States president 4. Tanks 5. The 18th century 6. Roman baths 7. The English Civil War 8. The Social Democratic Party 9. Abraham Lincoln 10. Argentina

QUIZ 243

. . . .

1 Who led the Afrika Korps in World War II?

2 What was his nickname?

3 Which British leader became famous for his rousing wartime speeches?

4 In which year were the Munich Olympics held?

5 Which German first started European printing with type?

6 Whose tomb was opened to much acclaim in 1922?

7 Who was the leader of the archaeological expedition to the site?

8 Who sailed in the *Mayflower*?

9 What was the Black Death?

10 In which century did it occur?

ANSWERS

1. General Rommel 2. The Desert Fox 3. Winston Churchill 4. 1968
5. Johannes Gutenberg 6. Tutankhamun 7. Howard Carter 8. The Pilgrim Fathers 9. Bubonic plague that swept Europe 10. 14th century

QUIZ 244

. . . .

1 Who sailed in the *Beagle*?

2 How many years did Deng Xiaopeng rule China for?

3 Who became Lord Protector of England in 1653?

4 What was the name given to the North's forces in the American Civil War?

5 What was the largest amphitheatre in Roman times?

6 Was its capacity: 3000, 11,000, 20,000 or 50,000?

7 At which London Underground station did 31 people lose their lives in 1987?

8 What did Queen Victoria celebrate in 1887?

9 Why did the ancient Chinese bury jade objects with the dead?

10 What name was given to the South's forces in the American Civil War?

ANSWERS

1. Charles Darwin 2. 20 3. Oliver Cromwell 4. Union 5. The Colosseum
6. 50,000 7. King's Cross 8. Her golden jubilee (50 years as Queen) 9. They
believed jade protected and preserved the dead body 10. Confederate

QUIZ 245

- -

1. What does the 'VJ' in VJ Day stand for?

2. Of what were the Lancaster, the Heinkel He-111 and the Liberator all examples?

3. How did Joan of Arc die?

4. Who led the Gunpowder Plot?

5. What caused the *Titanic* to sink in 1912?

6. Which monarch reigned longest in Britain?

7. What was the name of the airships that bombed London in 1915?

8. On which Japanese city was the first atom bomb dropped?

9. Who built Ermine Street and Fosse Way?

10. In what year did Japan bomb Pearl Harbor?

ANSWERS

1. Victory in Japan 2. World War II bomber aircraft 3. She was burned at the stake 4. Guy Fawkes 5. Hitting an iceberg 6. Queen Victoria 7. Zeppelins 8. Hiroshima 9. The Romans 10. 1941

QUIZ 246

. . . .

1   What was the nickname given to the German's
    sustained bombing campaign of London and
    other British cities during World War II?

2   Which two royal houses fought the War of the
    Roses?

3   Which ship was sunk at the Battle of the River
    Plate?

4   Whom did Mary Tudor marry while Queen of
    England?

5   In the English Civil War, what was the name given
    to the anti-royalist forces?

6   Who was king of England immediately before
    Henry VIII?

7   Who did William of Normandy defeat at the Battle
    of Hastings?

8   Which general led the North's forces in the
    American Civil War?

9   How many times was Harold Wilson elected
    prime minister?

10 In which year was there a General Strike in Britain:
    1906, 1916, 1926 or 1936?

ANSWERS

1. The Blitz 2. York and Lancaster 3. *Graf Spee* 4. King Philip II of Spain
5. The roundheads 6. King Henry VII 7. King Harold 8. Ulysses S. Grant
9. Two 10. 1926

QUIZ 247

. . . .

1 In which year was the Panama Canal officially opened: 1876, 1906 or 1914?

2 Who was the last Russian tsar?

3 What happened to him and his family in 1917?

4 Who made the famous Gettysberg address in 1863?

5 Which boy band comprises Harry Judd, Danny Jones, Dougie Poynter and Tom Fletcher?

6 Which royal house followed the Tudors?

7 Which country offered Albert Einstein its presidency in 1948?

8 Which country did Nikita Khrushchev lead in the 1950s?

9 Which sports did the Scots government ban in 1467?

10 Which military leader was born in Corsica in 1769 and became Emperor of France in 1804?

ANSWERS

1. 1914 2. Nikolaus II 3. They were executed 4. Abraham Lincoln 5. McFly
6. The House of Stuart 7. Israel 8. The Soviet Union 9. Football and golf
10. Napoleon

QUIZ 248

1 Which ancient Egyptian sculpture is the largest ancient sculpture still in existence?

2 Gary Kasparov lost a famous chess contest in 1997; name the winner.

3 How many British general elections were there in 1974?

4 Which material, beginning with P, did the ancient Egyptians write on?

5 What was the name given to the people who wrote in ancient Egyptian times?

6 Which wife of Henry VIII gave birth to Mary Tudor?

7 How many years was Henry married to this queen: two, four, eight or twenty-four?

8 With which continent is the explorer Robert Falcon Scott associated?

9 Which historic city is a holy place for three different religions: Mecca, Jerusalem or Baghdad?

10 What happened to the explorers Francis Drake, Captain James Cook and David Livingstone on their expeditions?

ANSWERS

1. The Sphinx 2. Deep Blue – a computer 3. Two 4. Papyrus 5. Scribes
6. Catherine of Aragon 7. Twenty-four 8. Antarctica 9. Jerusalem (Christian, Muslim and Jewish) 10. They all died whilst exploring

QUIZ 249

- -

1   What name was given to the Spanish fleet that set sail to invade England in 1588?

2   Who ruled England at the time?

3   Who was president of the United States during World War I?

4   King Alfred the Great defended large parts of Britain from invasion by whom?

5   Who became the first woman Speaker of the House of Commons in 1992?

6   Who was 'Monty' of the Desert Rats?

7   Which aircraft carrier was sunk off the coast of Gibraltar in 1941?

8   What did Caligula, Augustus and Titus all have in common?

9   Which royal house followed the House of Stuart?

10 The last execution of a witch in England took place in which year: 980, 1406 or 1712?

ANSWERS

1. The Spanish Armada 2. Queen Elizabeth I 3. Woodrow Wilson 4. Vikings
5. Betty Boothroyd 6. Field Marshall Montgomery 7. HMS *Ark Royal* 8. They were all Roman emperors 9. Hanover 10. 1712

QUIZ 250

. . . .

1 In 1936, a march protesting about unemployment set off from which northern town?

2 Which famous Indian leader was known as The Mahatma, meaning 'great soul'?

3 Which scrolls were discovered in caves in Jordan in 1947?

4 Which South American country did Pizarro conquer in 1533?

5 Of which political party was Benjamin Disraeli the leader during the Victorian era?

6 Which religion was directly influenced by the prophet Muhammad in the AD600s?

7 Which religion was introduced into Japan in 552?

8 What type of machine were the R101 and the Hindenberg, both built in the 1930s?

9 Which revolt did Wat Tyler lead in 1381?

10 Which two Bolshevik leaders seized power in Russia in 1917?

ANSWERS

1. Jarrow 2. Gandhi 3. The Dead Sea Scrolls 4. Peru 5. The Tory Party
6. Islam 7. Buddhism 8. Passenger airships 9. The Peasants' Revolt 10. Lenin
and Trotsky

QUIZ 251

• •

1   Members and supporters of CND marched in 1958, what does CND stand for?

2   At the end of which war was the United Nations formed?

3   In which year were the first free elections in South Africa held?

4   Mao Zedong led the Communists to power in which country?

5   In which year was he made president of that country: 1936, 1949 or 1964?

6   Was General Patton British, German, American or Italian?

7   Which country did Cleopatra rule?

8   Which Asian war took place between 1965 and 1973?

9   What did the suffragettes campaign for?

10 Which famous army leader was known as the Iron Duke?

ANSWERS

1. Campaign for Nuclear Disarmament 2. World War II 3. 1994 4. China
5. 1949 6. American 7. Ancient Egypt 8. The Vietnam War 9. Votes for
women 10. Duke of Wellington

QUIZ 252

• •

1. Which American president was assassinated in 1963?

2. Who replaced him as the United States leader?

3. Which language was spoken by the ancient Romans?

4. Which African country did Italy invade in 1935?

5. What was a hoplite: a Greek foot soldier, a Saxon battleaxe or a sacred Norman drinking vessel?

6. Which leader described an 'iron curtain' descending across Europe?

7. Which event was recorded as first taking place in 776BC at Olympia?

8. Which country was known as Gaul in Roman times?

9. The first college of which university was established in 1249?

10. Which FBI chief died in 1972 after serving eight presidents?

ANSWERS

1. John F Kennedy 2. Lyndon Johnson 3. Latin 4. Abyssinia 5. A Greek foot soldier 6. Winston Churchill 7. The Olympic Games 8. France 9. Oxford University 10. J Edgar Hoover

QUIZ 253

• •

1 Who was the leader responsible for Cambodia's 'killing fields' of the 1970s?

2 What were a cross-staff and astrolabe used for?

3 Which king started the Hundred Years' War with France?

4 Who completed the first known round-the-world voyage?

5 From which country did he come?

6 In which century did he achieve the feat?

7 What was the name of Columbus' flagship when he first crossed the Atlantic?

8 Which country in the British Empire mutinied in 1857?

9 In which modern-day country did the Assyrians live: Israel, Turkey, Morocco or Iraq?

10 Ssu Tsung was the last emperor of which Chinese dynasty?

ANSWERS

1. Pol Pot 2. Navigation 3. Edward III 4. Ferdinand Magellan 5. Portugal
6. The 16th century 7. Santa Maria 8. India 9. Iraq 10. Ming

QUIZ 254

. . . .

1 Which two countries fought the Battle of Agincourt?

2 Which word is used to describe the murder of six million Jews in the period 1939–45?

3 What was the name of the German air force in World War II?

4 In which culture was Zeus considered the king of the gods?

5 Romulus Augustulus was the last what?

6 Egbert was the first British king to be converted to what?

7 What was a guillotine?

8 In which revolution was it first used?

9 Idi Amin was the dictator of which African country?

10 Which notorious Australian robber was hanged at Melbourne in 1880?

ANSWERS

1. France and England 2. The Holocaust 3. Luftwaffe 4. The ancient Greeks
5. Roman emperor 6. Christianity 7. A device for beheading people 8. The
French Revolution 9. Uganda 10. Ned Kelly

QUIZ 255

1 In 1637, Japan banned all foreigners apart from one country: which one?

2 In which decade was the Korean war fought?

3 What day did June 4, 1944, become known as?

4 Who shot John F Kennedy and then was shot dead himself days later?

5 Belgium declared itself independent in 1831, from which country?

6 In which year was Britain given a 99-year lease on Hong Kong?

7 In the Trojn wars, which side used a wooden horse to enter the city of Troy?

8 Germany and Japan were two of the main Axis powers in World War II; can you name another?

9 What was Valhalla to the Vikings?

10 What nickname was given to Mary Tudor, Queen of England between 1583 and 1588?

ANSWERS

1. The Netherlands 2. The 1950s 3. D-Day 4. Lee Harvey Oswald 5. The Netherlands 6. 1898 7. The Greeks 8. Italy (also Bulgaria and Romania) 9. The hall of the gods, where warriors who died in battle went 10. Bloody Mary

QUIZ 256

● ●

1 Who was emperor of Japan during World War II?

2 The first passenger railway opened in 1825 between which two English towns?

3 Who was commander-in-chief of the Southern forces in the American Civil War?

4 Over the ownership of which two states did the US and Mexico fight in 1846–48?

5 Which 2004 film sequel is subtitled *Destination London*?

6 Who was the first prime minister of England?

7 What was the system of racial segregation in South Africa called?

8 How many Conservative prime ministers of Britain have there been since 1950?

9 Who was the last British king to die in battle?

10 What deadly weapon was first used at the Battle of Ypres in 1915?

ANSWERS

1. Hirohito 2. Stockton and Darlington 3. General Robert E Lee
4. Texas and California 5. *Agent Cody Banks* 6. Sir Robert Walpole
7. Apartheid 8. Seven 9. Richard III 10. Chlorine gas

QUIZ 257

• •

1. Which American political party did President Jimmy Carter represent: Republican or Democrat?

2. Which vegetable is Sir Walter Raleigh believed to have brought back from the Americas?

3. Which countries did Captain James Cook explore on his first long-distance voyage?

4. Who was the Liberal Party leader before Charles Kennedy?

5. Who was the famous gangster responsible for the St Valentine's Day Massacre?

6. What was a blunderbuss: a methodist preacher, a type of gun or an early steam locomotive?

7. With which terrorist group is the political party, Sinn Fein, linked?

8. Pudding Lane in London was the starting point for which disaster in the 1600s?

9. In which decade was the first test-tube baby born?

10. Offa's Dyke was built in England in the AD700s to keep out the people of which country?

ANSWERS

1. Democrat 2. The potato 3. Australia and New Zealand 4. Paddy Ashdown 5. Al Capone 6. A type of gun 7. The IRA 8. The Great Fire of London 9. The 1970s 10. The Welsh

QUIZ 258

. . . .

1 Which country joined World War I in April 1917?

2 Which king was the first to become head of the Church of England?

3 Who was the first Labour prime minister?

4 The Gunpowder Plot was an attempt to assassinate whom?

5 The Treaty of Versailles was signed after which war?

6 Which king of England was forced by the country's barons to sign Magna Carta?

7 Whose forces were defeated at the Battle of Actium?

8 In which year was Dachau, the first Nazi concentration camp, established?

9 In 1979, which country was invaded by Soviet troops?

10 Which famous explorer died in poverty in 1506?

ANSWERS

1. The United States 2. Henry VIII 3. James Ramsey MacDonald 4. King James I 5. World War I 6. King John 7. Cleopatra and Mark Antony 8. 1933 9. Afghanistan 10. Christopher Columbus

QUIZ 259

• •

1   Which island people killed Captain Cook in 1779?

2   What did the Luddites protest against?

3   The Gunpowder Plotters, led by Guy Fawkes, rolled
    36 barrels of explosives underneath which
    building?

4   What did the term SALT stand for in the 1970s
    and 1980s?

5   What happened to the boat *Rainbow Warrior* in
    1985?

6   Who owned the boat?

7   On which island was Napoleon exiled for the last
    six years of his life?

8   What do the initials PLO stand for?

9   What opened between Paddington and
    Farringdon Street in 1863?

10 What was cosmonaut Aleksei Leonov the first
    to do?

ANSWERS

1. The Hawaiian islanders 2. The factory conditions and machinery of the
Industrial Revolution 3. The Houses of Parliament 4. Strategic Arms
Limitation Talks 5. It was blown up by the French secret service
6. Greenpeace 7. St Helena 8. Palestine Liberation Organization
9. The world's first underground railway 10. Walk in space

QUIZ 260

1 Benito Mussolini ruled which European country in the 1900s?

2 Did his rule end in the 1930s, 1940s or 1970s?

3 Which country did Russia sell Alaska to?

4 The potato famine struck which country in the period 1845–46?

5 Live Aid was a charity concert in aid of which famine-stricken African country: Rwanda, Ethiopia or Morocco?

6 Was Live Aid held in 1978, 1985, 1990 or 1992?

7 King George VI was the father of which member of the British royal family?

8 King James I had which famous explorer executed: Sir Francis Drake, Sir Walter Raleigh or Sir Francis Chichester?

9 What sort of weapon did China first test in the 1970s?

10 Did the ancient Greeks, Egyptians or Romans build the Sphinx?

ANSWERS

1. Italy 2. 1940s 3. The United States 4. Ireland 5. Ethiopia 6. 1985
7. Queen Elizabeth II 8. Sir Walter Raleigh 9. Nuclear bomb 10. Ancient Egyptians

QUIZ 261

· ·

1   What does a thermometer measure?

2   What is a Triceratops an example of?

3   Which precious metal and element has the atomic symbol Ag?

4   What is a half plus an eighth?

5   Which planet is nearest to the Sun?

6   What did Orville and Wilbur Wright successfully build?

7   Which planet did the two Viking spacecraft land on?

8   What is 50 percent of 122?

9   How many sides does a triangle have?

10 Which British and French plane was the only supersonic (faster-than-sound) airliner in service?

ANSWERS

1. Temperature 2. A dinosaur 3. Silver 4. Five-eighths 5. Mercury 6. The first heavier-than-air aircraft 7. Mars 8. 61 9. Three 10. Concorde

QUIZ 262

• •

1   What is the longest side of a triangle called?

2   What scientific device did Dutch spectacle-maker Hans Lippershey invent?

3   How much is 35 percent of 300?

4   At what temperature in centigrade does water boil?

5   What type of triangle has three sides of equal length?

6   Which British engineer is associated with the invention of the jet engine?

7   Which element has the chemical symbol Fe?

8   How do you write 1.5 as a vulgar fraction?

9   What happens to an object if it accelerates?

10 What can you tell from the rings of a tree trunk?

ANSWERS

1. The hypotenuse 2. The telescope 3. 105 4. 100 degrees 5. An equilateral triangle 6. Sir Frank Whittle 7. Iron 8. 3/2 9. Its speed increases 10. The age of the tree

QUIZ 263

. . . .

1 Which famous table did Russian Dmitri Mendeleév produce?

2 What number did an Indian by the name of Vyas invent in the AD600s?

3 Which computer input device was invented by Douglas Englebart?

4 Which planet did astronomer William Herschel discover?

5 What does Vitamin D help to keep strong and healthy?

6 What important computer component was invented in 1970–71?

7 What takes 247.7 years to orbit the Sun?

8 Which geological era lasted for 135 million years and is commonly called the age of the reptiles?

9 Was the Jurassic period part of the above era?

10 How many stars are estimated to be in the Milky Way: 20 billion, 200 million or 200 billion?

ANSWERS

1. The periodic table of elements 2. Zero 3. The mouse 4. Uranus 5. Bones and teeth 6. The microprocessor 7. Pluto 8. Mesozoic 9. Yes 10. 200 billion

QUIZ 264

- -

1 How many grammes are there in a kilogram?

2 Does hot air travel up or down?

3 Which element has the chemical symbol O?

4 What does the North pole of a magnet do?

5 How many threes are in 39?

6 Which planet is known as the red planet?

7 How many sides has a pentagon?

8 Which computer game family own pet cats called Phoebe and Azrael?

9 Which raw material is most plastic made from?

10 What is 100 divided by four?

ANSWERS

1. 1,000 2. Up 3. Oxygen 4. Point to magnetic north 5. 13 6. Mars 7. Five
8. The Sims 9. Oil 10. 25

QUIZ 265

. . . .

1 Which ancient Greek had a theorem about triangles?

2 Of what are COBOL, FORTRAN and LISP examples?

3 Who invented the lightning conductor?

4 Which vitamin helps fight disease?

5 Which part of a car can come in disc and drum form?

6 Which electronic device was first developed in 1948 by Walter Brattain and others?

7 Which planet has 12 satellites or moons?

8 Who developed a General Theory of Relativity?

9 How many bits in a byte?

10 What was NASA's *Columbia* the first example of?

ANSWERS

1. Pythagoras 2. Computer languages 3. Benjamin Franklin 4. Vitamin A
5. Brakes 6. The transistor 7. Jupiter 8. Albert Einstein 9. Eight
10 The space shuttle

QUIZ 266

. . . .

1 There are three elements that can be magnetised. Iron is one – name the other two.

2 What is the more common name for sodium chloride?

3 Which Danish astronomer had a nose made out of silver and wax?

4 What machine first worked for a living in 1961?

5 Did Puma, Unimation or AEG make that machine?

6 How many degrees do the angles in a pentagon add up to?

7 What is the average human body temperature?

8 How many hours are there in a week?

9 What part of an atom did Ernest Rutherford discover in 1919?

10 What does the scientific abbreviation r.p.m. stand for?

ANSWERS

1. Nickel and Cobalt 2. Table salt 3. Tycho Brahe 4. Robot 5. Unimation
6. 540 7. 37°C 8. 168 9. Proton 10. Revolutions per minute

QUIZ 267

· ·

1 What covers more than two thirds of the world's surface?

2 At room temperature, is helium a gas, a liquid or a solid?

3 How many degrees do the angles of a triangle add up to?

4 Which fruit fell on Sir Isaac Newton's head, making him aware of gravity?

5 Which paper is used to measure acids and alkalis?

6 If that paper is dipped in acid, what colour does it turn?

7 What were the Manchester Mark I and the Colossus early examples of?

8 What is the most common element in the Earth's atmosphere?

9 Alphabetically, which is the last planet in the Solar System?

10 What name was given to the American missions to the Moon?

ANSWERS

1. Water 2. A gas 3. 180 4. An apple 5. Litmus paper 6. Red 7. Computers
8. Nitrogen 9. Uranus 10. Apollo

QUIZ 268

● ●

1 What does a van der Graaf generator create?

2 What does the term AI stand for?

3 What is the base two number system more commonly known as?

4 Who invented the process for freezing food?

5 Can lightning strike in the same place twice?

6 Which important gas did Joseph Priestley discover in 1774?

7 What type of boat has one or more sets of wings underwater which help lift much of the craft above the water?

8 Which two metals is solder largely a mixture of?

9 How many sides does a rhombus have?

10 What does the Mohs scale measure?

ANSWERS

1. Static electricity 2. Artificial Intelligence 3. Binary 4. Clarence Birdseye
5. Yes 6. Oxygen 7. Hydrofoil 8. Lead and tin 9. Four 10. Hardness of a
material

QUIZ 269

• •

1   Which word describes the path travelled by a body in space?

2   What do you do if you 'boot up' a computer?

3   What is an oxide?

4   How is a black hole created?

5   Which synthetic fibre was invented by American chemist Wallace Carothers?

6   Which part of the body secretes the hormone insulin?

7   Is the element mercury a solid, a liquid or a gas at room temperature?

8   If a material is said to be ductile, what can be done to it?

9   What is desalination?

10 What is dilute acetic acid better known as?

ANSWERS

1. Orbit 2. Start it 3. A compound of oxygen and another element 4. By a massive star collapsing in on itself 5. Nylon 6. The pancreas 7. A liquid 8. It can be drawn into thin wires 9. Producing fresh water by removing salt from sea water 10. Vinegar

QUIZ 270

. . . .

1   Which type of engine are turboshafts and turbofans examples of?

2   How many centimetres in nine metres?

3   What name do we give to a portable store of electrical energy, sometimes known as a cell?

4   How many sides do quadrilaterals have?

5   What metal are most soft-drinks cans made of?

6   Which is the lightest element of all: helium, hydrogen or fluorine?

7   How long is a year on Saturn: 9, 79 or 29 Earth-years?

8   Who invented dynamite and gave his name to a famous series of prizes?

9   What does a pneumatic drill use to provide it with power?

10 Which piece of computing equipment can come in the form of dot matrix, laser and inkjet?

ANSWERS

1. Jet engine 2. 900 3. Battery 4. Four 5. Aluminium 6. Hydrogen 7. 29
8. Alfred Nobel 9. Air 10. Printer

QUIZ 271

1   In base two numbers, what do you get by adding 11 and 1?

2   Which first example of this device filled a hall 140 square metres and weighed 30 tonnes?

3   What does Halley's Comet do every 76 years?

4   Who performed the first-ever heart transplant operation?

5   What does a Geiger counter measure?

6   Does sound travel faster through air or water?

7   What are the three states of matter?

8   What name is given to people who break into a computer system without permission?

9   Which insect transmits the disease malaria?

10 What makes Dolly the sheep so special?

ANSWERS

1. 100 2. Computer 3. Completes its orbit around the Sun 4. Dr Christiaan Barnard 5. Radioactivity 6. Through water 7. Solid, liquid and gas
8. Hackers 9. The mosquito 10. It was the first mammal to be cloned from another adult mammal

QUIZ 272

. . . .

1 What is the hardest naturally occurring substance?

2 Does a star implode or explode to become a black hole?

3 What does the computer term RAM stand for?

4 Which American inventor counts the electric light and sound recording amongst his inventions?

5 What is an ore?

6 Which important metal can be obtained from the ores hematite and magnetite?

7 Who was the first woman in space?

8 What is the unit of electrical current called?

9 What is calcium carbonate commonly known as?

10 What device did Elisha Otis invent in 1853?

ANSWERS

1. Diamond 2. Implode 3. Random Access Memory 4. Thomas Alva Edison
5. A mineral from which metals can be obtained 6. Iron 7. Valentina
Tereshkova 8. The ampere (or amp) 9. Chalk 10. The lift or elevator

QUIZ 273

• •

1 Which number is bigger: a: 8 x 7 or b: 63 – 8?

2 Which planet is the largest in our Solar System?

3 How many sides has a hexagon?

4 Which arithmetical aid did Sir Clive Sinclair first sell in 1973?

5 What is a machine for burning large amounts of rubbish called?

6 Do magnets with different poles facing attract or repel?

7 What did Igor Sikorsky do in 1939?

8 What is 30 percent of 120?

9 Which type of space instrument was named after Edwin Hubble?

10 How many sides does a snowflake have?

ANSWERS

1. a (8 x 7 = 56 while 63–8 = 55) 2. Jupiter 3. Six 4. Electronic calculator
5. An incinerator 6. Attract 7. Build the world's first helicopter 8. 36
9. A telescope 10. Six

QUIZ 274

• •

True or false:

1 Some museums have robot security guards patrolling their floors.

2 The aircraft *Voyager* flew for nine days without refuelling to travel around the world.

3 The oldest known living person reached 149 years of age.

4 A fax page is made up of as many as six million individual dots.

5 If your body temperature reaches 30 degrees centigrade, you will fall unconscious.

6 You use over 200 muscles when you walk.

7 The gravity on Jupiter is 318 times stronger than on Earth.

8 There are canals on Mars.

9 Robodoc is a surgical assistant robot with over 1,000 successful operations under its belt.

10 1968 saw the launch of the first spacecraft.

ANSWERS

1. True 2. True 3. False 4. True 5. True 6. True 7. True 8. False 9. True
10. False

QUIZ 275

• •

1 On which planet did the *Pathfinder* mission land in 1996?

2 What do the letters DC stand for in electricity?

3 What is measured in millibars?

4 Which term is used to describe the amount of matter in an object?

5 What are the three primary colours of light?

6 If the base of a triangle is 3 cm and its height 4cm, what is its area?

7 In the base two number system what does 1011+10 equal?

8 Who hosted the long-running astronomy show *The Sky at Night*?

9 What term describes the change in shape or size of an object when a force is applied to squash or stretch it?

10 Which element has the chemical symbol Na?

ANSWERS

1. Mars 2. Direct Current 3. Atmospheric pressure 4. Mass 5. Red, blue and green 6. 6 cm 7. 1101 8. Patrick Moore 9. Elasticity 10. Sodium

QUIZ 276

• •

1 Do magnets with the same poles facing each other repel or attract?

2 What is white spirit made from: petroleum, plant fibres or diluted mercury?

3 What type of power station splits atoms to create electricity?

4 Is a kilogram more or less than two pounds?

5 Which planet is most famous for its rings?

6 Which common device did Laszlo Biro of Argentina invent in 1944?

7 What is the second most common element in air?

8 Are all metals magnetic?

9 Which body in our Solar System is 330,000 times bigger than Earth and only a quarter as dense?

10 How much of a cake is left if you eat $^4/_8$ of it?

ANSWERS

1. Attract 2. Petroleum 3. A nuclear power station 4. More 5. Saturn 6. The ballpoint pen 7. Oxygen 8. No, only three 9. The Sun 10. Half of it

QUIZ 277

· ·

1 What does the abbreviation NASA stand for?

2 What is the length of the outer edge of a circle better known as?

3 Which colour reflects heat better: black or white?

4 What is the ohm a measurement of?

5 Which planet is the closest in size to Earth?

6 Which term describes the atoms of two or more elements bonded together by a chemical reaction?

7 Is an electron a positive or negatively charged particle of an atom?

8 Who was the first person in space?

9 What do the letters AC stand for in electricity?

10 Which planet did the space probe *Mariner 10* pass three times?

ANSWERS

1. National Aeronautics and Space Administration 2. Circumference
3. White 4. Electrical resistance 5. Venus 6. Compound 7. Negatively
charged 8. Yuri Gagarin 9. Alternating Current 10. Mercury

QUIZ 278

• •

1 What is another name for solid carbon dioxide?

2 Which female scientist won a Nobel prize for chemistry for her work investigating radioactivity?

3 Which element is present in every organic compound?

4 What were Skylab and Salut early examples of?

5 What is the glowing piece of wire in a light bulb called?

6 What metal is that wire commonly made from?

7 What is the force of flight that moves an aircraft forward?

8 What is the force of flight that pulls an aircraft back?

9 What is a catalyst in chemistry?

10 What connects the literary characters of Bridget Jones and Adrian Mole?

ANSWERS

1. Dry ice 2. Marie Curie 3. Carbon 4. Space stations 5. The filament
6. Tungsten 7. Thrust 8. Drag 9. A substance that changes the rate of
a chemical reaction 10. Both are famed for writing diaries

QUIZ 279

. . . .

1   With what sort of power are the engineers James Watt and Thomas Newcomen associated?

2   Which part of a computer is sometimes called a VDU?

3   Is the radius of a circle bigger or smaller than the circle's diameter?

4   In which industry would you find a rig, tankers and a refinery?

5   What is the symbol for the chemical element Nitrogen?

6   As a fraction, how much is 25 percent of something?

7   How much more hydrogen than oxygen would you find in water?

8   What happened in space on July 20, 1969?

9   What is the solid form of water called?

10 How many poles does a permanent magnet have?

ANSWERS

1. Steam 2. A monitor or computer screen 3. Smaller (the radius is half the diameter) 4. The oil industry 5. N 6. $1/4$ 7. Twice as much 8. Men reached the Moon 9. Ice 10. Two

QUIZ 280

. . . .

1 Which is the second largest planet in the Solar System?

2 Is there any air on the Moon?

3 In which year did the first space shuttle fly?

4 What mineral rates one on the Mohs scale?

5 Carbohydrates contain three elements: carbon and oxygen are two, what is the third?

6 What is an alloy?

7 John Logie Baird is associated with the invention of which machine?

8 What is the term 'maglev' short for?

9 What is the term used to describe a substance changing from a liquid to a gas?

10 Does a convex surface bend inwards or outwards?

ANSWERS

1. Saturn 2. No 3. 1981 4. Talc 5. Hydrogen 6. A substance composed of two or more metals 7. Television 8. Magnetic levitation 9. Boiling point 10. Outwards

QUIZ 281

• •

1 Is the boiling point of silver higher than iron?

2 What is the name of the hole in your eye that lets in light?

3 In physics, what is the name given to a rod that turns around a fixed point?

4 What is the value of pi?

5 What uses about 40 percent of all silver?

6 What was the name of the rocket that propelled the Apollo missions to the moon?

7 What is a compact flash card?

8 What force of flight is generated by an aircraft's wings?

9 What types of energy does a light bulb give off?

10 Who invented the electric dynamo in 1831?

ANSWERS

1. No (Iron's boiling point is higher) 2. The pupil 3. A lever 4. 3.142
5. Camera film 6. *Saturn V* 7. A portable form of computer memory storage
8. Lift 9. Heat and light energy 10. Michael Faraday

QUIZ 282

• •

1   What is the name given to magnets powered by electricity?

2   When water becomes ice, does it expand or contract?

3   How many times does 9 go into 81?

4   What was the name of the first man on the Moon?

5   What was the name of the spacecraft that took him there?

6   Which metal is a good conductor of heat and electricity and is used in plumbing and wiring?

7   Which clothing device did Whitcomb Judson invent in 1892?

8   Did the United States, China or the USSR send the first satellite into space?

9   What was the name of that satellite?

10 Which part of a car engine sets fire to the petrol and air mixture in a cylinder?

ANSWERS

1. Electromagnets 2. Expand 3. Nine 4. Neil Armstrong 5. *Apollo 11*
6. Copper 7. The zip fastener 8. USSR 9. Sputnik 10. Spark plugs

QUIZ 283

. . . .

1. Which invention of James Martin made the lives of military jet pilots much safer?

2. What is the branch of science that studies metals called?

3. George Stephenson invented which form of transport?

4. Who was the second man on the Moon?

5. Which medical instrument is used to listen to the sounds within the body?

6. How long was the first aircraft flight: 12 seconds, 5 minutes or 11 minutes?

7. What are the names of the bones that make up the spine called?

8. Which two elements make up sand?

9. What does ISP mean in computing?

10. Who invented the first car driven by an internal combustion engine?

ANSWERS

1. The ejection seat 2. Metallurgy 3. The steam locomotive 4. Edwin 'Buzz' Aldrin 5. Stethoscope 6. 12 seconds 7. Vertebrae 8. Oxygen and silicon 9. Internet Service Provider 10. Karl Benz

QUIZ 284

• •

1   Celsius and Farenheit are two temperature scales: can you name another one?

2   In which country was the magnetic compass invented?

3   A polymer is a substance made of a chain of small molecules; what are these small molecules called?

4   If a material has the property of 'malleability' what does it mean?

5   Who invented the spinning jenny?

6   What is a vacuum?

7   Can light travel through a vacuum?

8   Deoxyribonucleic acid is better known by three capital letters; what are they?

9   Who discovered the structure of that substance?

10   Which is the lightest metal: lithium, titanium or silver?

ANSWERS

1. Kelvin 2. China 3. Monomers 4. It can be hammered and shaped into thin sheets 5. James Hargreaves 6. A space which is empty of air and any other molecules 7. Yes 8. DNA 9. Watson and Crick 10. Lithium

QUIZ 285

1 How many planets are there in our Solar System?

2 Which is the least dense state of matter?

3 What sort of vehicle did Sir Christopher Cockerell invent?

4 If you rub a balloon against a woolly sweater, what do you help generate?

5 What is the chemical symbol of the metal aluminium?

6 When water reaches boiling point, what does it become?

7 How many weeks are there in five years?

8 If two angles of a triangle add up to 140 degrees, what must the third angle be?

9 Which navigational device uses a magnet suspended or floating in a liquid?

10 Did plesiosaurs live in water, in the air or on land?

ANSWERS

1. Nine 2. Gas 3. The hovercraft 4. Static electricity 5. Al 6. Steam (water vapour) 7. 260 8. 40 degrees 9. A magnetic compass 10. In water

QUIZ 286

• •

1 Which planet did William Herschel discover in 1781?

2 Is a single year on this planet equal to four, 24 or 82 Earth years?

3 Which harmful substance is produced by burning fossil fuels and is a major cause of acid rain?

4 What is the corrosion of iron and steel commonly known as?

5 Which two metals make the alloy bronze?

6 What does the diameter of a circle multiplied by pi equal?

7 What is the meaning of the initials CAD?

8 Which D word is the study of forces and motion?

9 What was the first spacecraft with more than one crew member: *Gemini 1*, *Mercury 4* or *Voskhod 1*?

10 What is 0.125 expressed as a fraction?

ANSWERS

1. Uranus 2. 82 3. Sulphur dioxide 4. Rust 5. Copper and tin 6. The circumference of the circle 7. Computer Aided Design 8. Dynamics 9. *Voskhod 1* 10. 1/8 (one-eighth)

QUIZ 287

• •

1 What name is given to a triangle with three different length sides?

2 Which acid is found in the sting of an ant?

3 What radioactive element was discovered by the German Martin Klaproth in 1841?

4 Which term, beginning with B, is the chemical opposite to acids?

5 What is kaolin an alternative name for?

6 Which is the only letter not to appear anywhere on the periodic table of elements?

7 How long does it take for light from the Sun to travel to Earth?

8 How are the characters of Carmen and Juni Cortez collectively known in a series of action adventure movies?

9 Are the noble gases very reactive or unreactive?

10 Which colour flame is produced when a substance containing potassium is burned?

ANSWERS

1. Scalene 2. Formic acid 3. Uranium 4. Base 5. China clay 6. J 7. Five minutes 8. Spy Kids 9. Unreactive 10. Purple

QUIZ 288

. . . .

1 Was the dinosaur Brontosaurus a meat or plant eater?

2 How many days are there in seven weeks?

3 Which sort of vehicle were the *Stratocruiser*, the *HP42* and the *Vickers Viscount*?

4 Were they powered by jet or piston engines?

5 What is the chemical symbol for lead?

6 Is a palmtop computer larger or smaller than a notebook computer?

7 If three angles in a quadrilateral equal 300 degrees, what is the size of the fourth angle?

8 What are the three planets farthest away from the Sun?

9 What does a vacuum flask do to liquids?

10 What is the centre of an atom called?

ANSWERS

1. Plant eater 2. 49 3. Airliners 4. Piston engines 5. Pb 6. Smaller 7. 60 degrees 8. Uranus, Neptune and Pluto 9. Keeps them hot or cool 10. The nucleus

QUIZ 289

1 Which is heavier: 10 kilograms or 22 pounds?

2 In chemistry, what is centrifuging used for?

3 What is 240 volts in Britain and 110 volts in some other countries?

4 Is sound a form of energy?

5 Approximately how many grams would you find in an ounce?

6 What is 32 degrees Fahrenheit equal to in Centigrade?

7 How many planets in the solar system have a greater surface gravity than Earth?

8 Which colour flame does burning a substance containing calcium produce?

9 Which name is given to a triangle with two equal length sides?

10 Which computer peripheral would you use to transfer pages of text and pictures onto your computer?

ANSWERS

1. 10 kilograms 2. To separate out solid particles from a liquid 3. The household electricity supply 4. Yes 5. 28 6. Zero 7. Two: Jupiter and Neptune 8. Red 9. Isosceles 10. Scanner

QUIZ 290

• •

1 What does the term OCR stand for?

2 Who was the first woman to walk in space?

3 What device did Robert Watson-Watt invent in 1935?

4 What are the three things needed for combustion to occur?

5 Which unit is equal to a thousand million bytes?

6 What is pharmacology the study of?

7 Which important material is made with the help of a Bessemer converter?

8 What does carbon dioxide do to limewater?

9 A human being has 24, 30 or 46 chromosomes?

10 What did John Boyd Dunlop invent in 1888?

ANSWERS

1. Optical Character Recognition 2. Svetlana Savitskaya 3. Radar 4. Heat, fuel and oxygen 5. A gigabyte 6. Drugs 7. Steel 8. Turn it milky 9. 46 10. Pneumatic tyres

QUIZ 291

. . . .

1 What is measured using pH numbers?

2 What type of energy does a photovoltaic cell convert into electricity?

3 What colour flame is produced when a substance containing copper is burned?

4 Where would you find the patella bone in your body?

5 What do the initials VR stand for?

6 What is the smallest number divisible by both 3 and 4?

7 With what communications device would you associate the name of Marconi?

8 What does the plastic covering around an electric wire do?

9 Which planet was the last to be discovered?

10 What is the name of the rod on a car which joins two wheels together?

ANSWERS

1. Whether a substance is acid or alkali 2. Light energy 3. Bluish green 4. Kneecap 5. Virtual reality 6. 12 7. Radio 8. Insulates the wire and protects people when handling it 9. Pluto 10. The axle

QUIZ 292

1 What kind of light gives people suntans?

2 Yellow, orange, red and green are four colours of the spectrum; can you name the other three?

3 What was the *Bell X1* the first craft to do?

4 Who piloted the *Bell X1* on its historic flight?

5 Which machine is used to move a fluid?

6 Which space probe, named after a famous astronomer, travelled to Jupiter and four of its moons?

7 How many minutes are there in a day?

8 Name the only supersonic airliner to fly other than *Concorde*?

9 What is the main ingredient used in making glass?

10 If a substance tests as neutral, what number would it be given on the pH scale?

ANSWERS

1. Ultraviolet light 2. Blue, violet and indigo 3. Travel faster than the speed of sound 4. Chuck Yeager 5. A pump 6. Galileo 7. 1,440 8. *Tupolev Tu-144* 9. Sand 10. Seven

QUIZ 293

• •

1 Which comet orbits the Sun every 76 years?

2 What is an LED?

3 What kind of camera was invented by Edwin Land?

4 What are A, B, AB and O the four types of in humans?~

5 What is the chemical symbol of zinc?

6 What is the boiling point of water in Fahrenheit?

7 In computing, what do the initials CPU stand for?

8 What is another name for the base ten number system?

9 Which element comes in a number of forms including graphite?

10 In the base two number system, what is 10011 + 101?

ANSWERS

1. Halley's Comet 2. Light-emitting diode 3. The Polaroid instant camera
4. Blood groups 5. Zn 6. 212 degrees 7. Central Processing Unit 8. Decimal
9. Carbon 10. 11000

QUIZ 294

1 The Montgolfier Brothers were the first to build which sort of flying machine?

2 A tin can is made of a thin layer of tin over steel, copper or bronze?

3 What sort of machines were *Saturn V* and *Ariane 4*?

4 How many sevens are there in 28?

5 How many sides does a parallelogram have?

6 What sort of code uses just dots and dashes to spell out words?

7 Which temperature measuring device did famous astronomer Galileo invent?

8 What nationality was Galileo?

9 How many twenty pence chocolate bars could you buy with four pounds?

10 The study of shapes and angles is called algebra, calculus or geometry?

ANSWERS

1. Hot air balloon 2. Steel 3. Space rockets 4. Four 5. Four 6. Morse code
7. Thermometer 8. Italian 9. 20 10. Geometry

QUIZ 295

1 Which device, with the full name modulator-demodulator, is used to connect your computer to the Internet?

2 Which term describes the Moon coming between the Sun and the Earth, covering the Sun up from our view?

3 In computing, what do the initials ROM stand for?

4 Which machine can vary its density to travel underwater or on the water's surface?

5 What is a magneto?

6 What was sent across the Atlantic for the first time in 1901?

7 What gemstone was first produced artificially in 1955?

8 Which pair flew the Atlantic for the first time in 1919?

9 What does antifreeze do to water's freezing point?

10 Which broadcast radio waveband operates from 160–255 kHz?

ANSWERS

1. Modem 2. An eclipse 3. Read-Only Memory 4. A submarine or submersible 5. A simple form of electricity generator 6. Radio signals 7. Diamond 8. Alcock and Brown 9. It lowers it 10. Long wave

QUIZ 296

. . . .

1   What was the name of the first space probe to send back pictures of Venus?

2   Which vitamin, found in liver and green vegetables, helps with clotting blood?

3   Which substance's chemical name is calcium oxide?

4   Which household cleaning device was invented by Cecil Booth in 1901?

5   Can you convert the base two number 101 into base ten?

6   What is estimated to have occurred over 15,000 million years ago?

7   How big is one nanometre?

8   What does an ammeter measure?

9   What is an antiseptic?

10 What is geothermal energy?

ANSWERS

1. Venera 9 2. Vitamin K 3. Lime 4. Vacuum cleaner 5. Five 6. The Big Bang
7. One billionth of a metre 8. Electric current 9. A substance that kills or
prevents the growth of germs 10. Energy using volcanic heat from
beneath the ground

QUIZ 297

•••••••••••••••••••••••••••••

1 Which types of machine are the *EH101*, the *Sea King* and the *Chinook*?

2 Which part of a personal computer acts as a permanent store of the user's files and programs?

3 Which important fuel and raw material is measured in barrels?

4 What did Louis Blériot cross in his aircraft in 1909?

5 How many sides does a heptagon have?

6 To split an atom is called fusion or fission?

7 What do wind turbines produce at a wind farm?

8 Which is the second smallest planet in the solar system?

9 When clothes dry outside, which process, beginning with E, causes the water to disappear?

10 When molecules are heated do they move faster or slower?

ANSWERS

1. Helicopters 2. The hard disk 3. Oil 4. The English Channel 5. Seven
6. Fission 7. Electricity 8. Mercury 9. Evaporation 10. Faster

QUIZ 298

1 Which arch-enemy of Peter Pan was played by Dustin Hoffman on film?

2 Who wrote The Wind in the Willows?

3 What are the short pleated skirts associated with Scotland called?

4 Is the word no negative or positive?

5 Which wimple wearers live in convents?

6 What does a frogman wear on his feet?

7 What is the name of the largest castle in the capital city of Scotland?

8 What name is given to a 60th part of an hour?

9 What kind of animal is Brian in The Magic Roundabout?

10 What part of the body is treated by an optician?

ANSWERS

1. Captain Hook 2. Kenneth Grahame 3. Kilts 4. Negative 5. Nuns
6. Flippers 7. Edinburgh Castle 8. A minute 9. A snail 10. The eyes